Action For A Change

To the students of Oregon and Minnesota,
who created the first PIRGs,
and to students nationwide,
who will create many more,
we dedicate this book.

A STUDENT'S MANUAL FOR PUBLIC INTEREST ORGANIZING

by RALPH NADER and DONALD ROSS
with Brent English and Joseph Highland

GROSSMAN PUBLISHERS   NEW YORK 1971

Action For
A Change

ACKNOWLEDGMENT

There are many other people who worked hard to make this book possible, and we are indebted to them. Foremost among them is James D. Welch, a Washington, D.C., attorney, whose nationwide travels helped bring the idea of Public Interest Research Groups to many campuses.

Special thanks also are due to Kate Blackwell and Brooks Van Ranson for editorial assistance, and to Eileen Kane, Connie Jo Smith, Bernadette Trabue, and Marsha Goodman for assistance in producing the manuscript.

Published in 1971 by Grossman Publishers
44 West 56th Street, New York, N.Y. 10019

Published simultaneously in Canada by
Fitzhenry and Whiteside, Ltd.

SBN 670-01936-4

Library of Congress Catalogue Card Number: 78-170617

Manufactured in the United States of America

CONTENTS

Part One

TOWARD AN
INITIATORY DEMOCRACY

This country has more problems than it should tolerate and more solutions than it uses. Few societies in the course of human history have faced such a situation: most are in the fires without the water to squelch them. Our society has the resources and the skills to keep injustice at bay and to elevate the human condition to a state of enduring compassion and creative fulfillment. How we go about using the resources and skills has consequences which extend well beyond our national borders to all the earth's people.

How do we go about this? The question has been asked and answered in many ways throughout the centuries. Somehow, the answers, even the more lasting ones, whether conforming or defiant, affect the reality of living far less than the intensity of their acceptance would seem to indicate. Take the conventional democratic creeds, for example. Many nations have adopted them, and their principles have wide popular reception. But the theories are widely separated from practice.

3

Power and wealth remain concentrated, decisions continue to be made by the few, victims have little representation in thousands of forums which affect their rights, livelihoods, and futures. And societies like ours, which have produced much that is good, are developing new perils, stresses, and deprivations of unprecedented scope and increasing risk. As the technologies of war and economics become more powerful and pervasive, the future, to many people, becomes more uncertain and fraught with fear. Past achievements are discounted or depreciated as the quality of life drifts downward in numerous ways. General economic growth produces costs which register, like the silent violence of poverty and pollution, with quiet desperation, ignored by entrenched powers, except in their rhetoric.

But the large institutions' contrived nonaccountability, complex technologies, and blameworthy indifference have not gone unchallenged, especially by the young. The very magnitude of our problems has reminded them of old verities and taught them new values. The generation gap between parents and children is in part a difference in awareness and expectation levels. Parents remember the Depression and are thankful for jobs. The beneficiaries — their children — look for more meaningful work and wonder about those who still do not have jobs in an economy of plenty because of rebuffs beyond their control. Parents remember World War II and what the enemy could have done to America; children look on the Vietnam War and other similar wars and wonder what America has done to other people and what, consequently, she is doing to herself. To parents, the noxious plume from factory smokestacks was the smell of the payroll; children view such sights as symbols of our domestic chemical warfare that is contaminating the air, water, and soil now and for many years hence. Parents have a more narrow concept of neighborhood; children view Earth as a shaky ship requiring us all to be our brother's keeper, regardless of political boundaries.

In a sense, these themes, or many like them, have distinguished the split between fathers and sons for generations; very often the resolution is that the sons become like the fathers. The important point is not that such differences involve a statistically small number of the young—historic changes, including the American Revolution, have always come through minorities—but that conditions are indeed serious, and a new definition of work is needed to deal with them.

That new kind of work is a new kind of citizenship. The word "citizenship" has a dull connotation—which is not surprising, given its treatment by civics books and the way it has been neglected. But the role of the citizen is obviously central to democracy, and it is time to face up to the burdens and liberations of citizenship.

Democratic systems are based on the principle that all power comes from the people. The administration of governmental power begins to erode this principle in practice immediately. The inequality of wealth, talent, ambition, and fortune in the society works its way into the governmental process which is supposed to be distributing even-handed justice, resources, and opportunities. Can the governmental process resist such pressures as the chief trustee of structured democratic power given it by the consent of the governed? Only to the degree to which the governed develop ways to apply their generic power in meticulous and practical ways on a continual basis. A citizenship of wholesale delegation and abdication to public and private power systems, such as prevails now, makes such periodic checks as elections little more than rituals. It permits tweedledum and tweedledee choices that put mostly indistinguishable candidates above meaningful issues and programs. It facilitates the overwhelming dominance of the pursuit of private or special interests, to the detriment of actions bringing the greatest good to the greatest number. It breeds despair, discouragement, resignation, cynicism, and all that is involved in the "You can't fight City Hall" syndrome. It constructs a society which has thousands of full-time manicurists and pastry-makers but less than a dozen citizen-specialists fighting full time against corporate water contamination or to get the government to provide food (from bulging warehouses) for millions of undernourished Americans.

Building a new way of life around citizenship action must be the program of the immediate future. The ethos that looks upon citizenship as an avocation or opportunity must be replaced with the commitment to citizenship as an obligation, a continual receiver of our time, energy, and skill. And that commitment must be transformed into a strategy of action that develops instruments of change while it focuses on what needs to be done. This is a critical point. Too often, people who are properly outraged over injustice concentrate so much on decrying the abuses and demanding the desired reforms that they never build the instruments to accomplish their objectives in a lasting manner.

There are three distinct roles through which effective citizenship activity can be channeled. First is the full-time professional citizen, who makes his career by applying his skills to a wide range of public problems. These citizens are not part of any governmental, corporate, or union institutions. Rather they are independently based, working *on* institutions to improve and reshape them or replace them with improved ways of achieving just missions. With their full-time base, they are able to mobilize and encourage part-time citizen activity.

With shorter workweeks heading toward the four-day week, part-time involvement can become an integral part of the good life for blue- and white-collar workers. Certainly many Americans desire to find the answers to two very recurrent questions: "What can I do to improve my community?" and "How do I go about doing it?" The development of the mechanics of taking a serious abuse, laying it bare before the public, proposing solutions, and generating the necessary coalitions to see these solutions through—these steps metabolize the latent will of people to contribute to their community and count as individuals rather than as cogs in large organizational wheels.

The emergence of capabilities and outlets for citizenship

expression has profound application to the third form of
citizenship activity—on-the-job citizenship. Consider the
immense knowledge of waste, fraud, negligence, and other
misdeeds which employees of corporations, governmental
agencies, and other bureaucracies possess. Most of this
country's abuses are secrets known to thousands of in-
siders, at times right down to the lowest paid worker. A
list of Congressional exposures in the poverty, defense,
consumer fraud, environmental, job safety, and regulatory areas over the past five years would substantiate
that observation again and again. The complicity of
silence, of getting along by going along, of just taking
orders, of "mum's the word" has been a prime target of
student activism and a prime factor leading students to
exercise their moral concern. When large organizations
dictate to their employees, and when their employees, in
turn, put ethical standards aside and perform their work
like minions—that is a classic prescription for institutional irresponsibility. The individual must have an opportunity and a right to blow the whistle on his organization—to make higher appeals to outside authorities, to
professional societies, to citizen groups—rather than be
forced to condone illegality, consumer hazards, oppression of the disadvantaged, seizure of public resources,
and the like. The ethical whistle-blower may be guided
by the Golden Rule, a refusal to aid and abet crimes,
occupational standards of ethics, or a geniune sense of
patriotism. To deny him or her the protections of the
law and supportive groups is to permit the institutional-

ization of organizational tyranny throughout the society at the grass roots where it matters.

On-the-job citizenship, then, is a critical source of information, ideas, and suggestions for change. Everybody who has a job knows of some abuses which pertain to that industry, commerce, or agency. Many would like to do something about these abuses, and their numbers will grow to the extent that they believe their assistance will improve conditions and not just expose them to being called troublemakers or threaten them with losing their jobs. They must believe that if they are right there will be someone to defend them and protect their right to speak out. A GM Fisher Body inspector went public on defectively welded Chevrolets that allowed exhaust gases, including carbon monoxide, to seep into passenger compartments. He had previously reported the defects repeatedly to plant managers without avail. In 1969 GM recalled over two million such Chevrolets for correction. The inspector still works at the plant, because union and outside supporters made it difficult for GM to reward such job citizenship with dismissal.

The conventional theory—that change by an institution in the public interest requires external pressure—should not displace the potential for change when that pressure forges an alliance with people of conscience *within* the institution. When the managerial elite knows that it cannot command its employees' complete allegiance to its unsavory practices, it will be far less likely to engage in such actions. This is a built-in check against the manager's disloyalty to the institution. Here is seen the significant nexus between full-time and part-time citizens with on-the-job citizens. It is a remarkable reflection on the underdevelopment of citizenship strategies that virtually no effort has been directed toward ending these divisions with a unison of action. But then, every occupation has been given expertise and full-time practitioners except the most important occupation of all—citizenship. Until unstructured citizen power is given the tools for impact, structured power, no matter how democratic in form, will tend toward abuse, indifference, or sloth. Such deterioration has occurred not only in supposedly democratic governments but in unions, cooperatives, motor clubs, and other membership groups. For organizations such as corporations, which are admittedly undemocratic (even toward their shareholders), the necessity for a professional citizenship is even more compelling.

How, then, can full-time, part-time, and on-the-job citizens work together on a wide, permanent, and effective scale? A number of models around the country, where young lawyers and other specialists have formed public interest firms to promote or defend citizen-consumer rights vis-à-vis government and corporate behavior, show the way. Given their tiny numbers and resources, their early impact has been tremendous. There are now a few dozen such people, but there need to be thousands, from all walks and experiences in life. What is demanded is a major redeployment of skilled manpower to make the commanding institutions in our society respond to needs which they have repudiated or neglected. This is a life's work for many Americans, and there is no reason why students cannot begin understanding precisely what is involved and how to bring it about.

It may be asked why the burden of such pioneering has to be borne by the young. The short answer is to say that this is the way it has always been. But there is a more functional reason: no other group is possessed of such flexibility, freedom, imagination, and willingness to experiment. Moreover, many students truly desire to be of service to humanity in practical, effective ways. The focused idealism of thousands of students in recent years brings a stronger realism to the instruments of student action outlined in this book. Indeed, this action program could not have been written in the fifties or early sixties. The world—especially the student world—has changed since those years.

Basic to the change is that victims of injustice are rising to a level of recurrent visibility. They are saying in many ways that a just system would allow, if not encourage victims to attain the power of alleviating their present suffering or future concerns. No longer is it possible to ignore completely the "Other America" of poverty, hunger, discrimination, and abject slums. Nor can the economic exploitation of the consumer be camouflaged by pompous references to the accumulation of goods and services in the American household. For the lines of responsibility between unsafe automobiles, shoddy merchandise, adulterated or denutritionized foods, and rigged prices with corporate behavior and governmental abdication have become far too clear. Similarly, environmental breakdowns have reached critical masses of destruction, despoilation, ugliness, and, above all, mounting health hazards through contaminated water, soil, and air. Growing protests by the most aggrieved have made more situations visible and have increased student perception of what was observed. Observation has led to participation which in turn has led to engagement. This sequence has most expressly been true for minorities and women. The aridity and seeming irrelevance of student course work has provided a backdrop for even more forceful rebounds into analyzing the way things are. Parallel with civil rights, antiwar efforts, ecology, and other campus causes, which have ebbed and flowed, the role of students within universities has become a stressful controversy which has matured many students and some faculty in a serious assessment of their relation to these institutions and to society at large.

This assessment illuminates two conditions. First, it takes too long to grow up in our culture. Extended adolescence, however it services commercial and political interests, deprives young people of their own fulfillment as citizens and of the chance to make valuable contributions to society. Second, contrary to the old edict that students should stay within their ivory tower before they go into the cold, cold world, there is every congruence between the roles of student and citizen. The old distinction will become even more artificial with the exercise and imaginative use of the eighteen- to twenty-year-old vote throughout the country.

For the first time, students will have decisive voting power in many local governments. One does not have to be a political science major to appreciate the depth of resourceful experience and responsibility afforded by such a role. The quality of electoral politics could be vastly improved, with direct impact on economic power blocs, if students use the vote intelligently and creatively around the country.

Such a happening is not a foregone conclusion, as those who fought successfully in the past for enfranchise-ment of other groups learned to their disappointment; but there are important reasons why this enfranchisement of the eighteen to twenty year old could be different. Over a third of the eleven and a half million people in this group are college students with a sense of identity and a geo-graphical concentration for canvassing and voting lever-age. Certainly, problems of communication are minimized, and a resurgent educational curriculum can be an intellectually demanding forum for treating the facts and programs which grow into issue-oriented politics in the students' voting capacities.

Full use of voting rights will induce a higher regard for students by older citizens, and elected and appointed officials. It is unlikely that legislators will rise on the floor of the legislature and utter the verbose ridicules wrapped in a smug authoritarian condescension that stu-

dents are accustomed to hearing. From now on, legislators will pay serious attention to students. Therefore the
student vote and the student citizen are intimately con-
nected. Student Public Interest Research Groups (PIRGs)
composed of full-time professional advocates and able
organizers recruited by and representing students as
citizens can have an enormous, constructive impact on
society. It could be a new ball game, if the student
players avoid the temptations of despair, dropping out,
and cynicism.

There are other obstacles which students put in their
own way that deserve candid appraisal by all those
involved in establishing and directing student PIRGs.
These are the shoals of personal piques, ego problems,
envy, megalomania, resentment, deception, and other
frailties which are distributed among students as they
are among other people. On such shoals the best
plan and the highest enthusiasm can run aground,
or be worn to exhaustion by the attrition of pettiness.
Even after the PIRGs are established, these frictions
can continue to frustrate and weaken their missions.
They will surface at every step—from recruitment to
choice of subject matters to the relations with the
PIRG professionals. They must be averted at every
step with candor, firmness, anticipatory procedures,
and a goal-oriented adhesion that reduces such inter-
ferences to nuisances. Such nuisances will serve to
remind all how important are character, stamina,
self-discipline, and consistency of behavior with the

values espoused to the success of the PIRG idea and its repercussive impact.

Self-discipline must be emphasized in this student age of free-think and free-do. Many kinds of cop-outs come in the garb of various liberated styles which sweep over campuses. Clearly, there has to be, for the purposes discussed in this volume, a reversal of the dictum: "If you desire to do it, you should do it" to "If you should do it, you should desire to do it." Such an attitude makes for persistence and incisiveness. It forces the asking of the important questions and the pursuit of the pertinent inquiries. It develops an inner reserve that refuses to give up and that thinks of ways for causes to be continually strengthened for sustained breakthroughs. The drive for a firmly rooted *initiatory* democracy is basic to all democratic participations and institutions, but initiatory democracy does not rest on the firmaments of wealth or bureaucratic power. It rests on conviction, work, intellect, values, and a willingness to sacrifice normal indulgences for the opportunity to come to grips as never before with the requisites of a just society. It also rests on a communion with the people for whom this effort is directed.

More and more students today are realistic about power, and they reject merely nominal democratic forms which shield or legitimize abuses. The great debates of the past over where power should be placed—in private or public hands—appear sterile to them. Students are suspicious of power wherever it resides because they know how such power can corrode and corrupt regardless of what crucible—corporate, governmental, or union—contains it. Moreover, the systematic use of public power by private interests against the citizenry, including the crude manipulation of the law as an instrument of oppression, has soured many of the brightest students against the efficacy of both government and law. At the same time, however, most· concerned students are averse to rigid ideological views which freeze intellects and narrow the choices of action away from adaptability and resiliency.

Such skepticism can become overextended in a form of self-paralysis. I have seen too many students downplay what other students have already accomplished in the past decade with little organization, less funds, and no support. Who began the sit-in movement in civil rights, a little over a decade ago, which led to rapid developments in the law? Four black engineering students. Who dramatized for the nation the facts and issues regarding the relentless environmental contamination in cities and rural America? Students. Who helped mobilize popular opposition to the continuance of the war in Vietnam and, at least, turned official policy toward withdrawal? Who focused attention on the need for change in university policies and obtained many of these changes? Who is enlarging the investigative tradition of the old muckrakers in the Progressive-Populist days at the turn of the century other than student teams of inquiry? Who is calling for and shaping a more relevant and empirical education that understands problems, considers solutions, and connects with people? Who poured on the pressure to get the eighteen- to twenty-year-old vote? A tiny minority of students.

Still the vast majority of their colleagues are languishing in colossal wastes of time, developing only a fraction of their potential, and woefully underpreparing themselves for the world they are entering in earnest. Student PIRGs can inspire with a large array of projects which demand the development of analytic and value training for and by students. These projects will show that knowledge and its uses are seamless webs which draw from all disciplines at a university and enrich each in a way that arranged interdisciplinary work can never do. The artificial isolations and ennui which embrace so many students will likely dissolve before the opportunity to relate education to life's quests, problems, and realities. The one imperative is for students to avoid a psychology of prejudgment in this period of their lives when most are as free to choose and act as they will ever be, given the constraints of careers and family responsibilities after graduation. The most astonishing aspect of what has to be done in this country by citizens is that it has never been tried. What students must do, in effect, is create their own careers in these undertakings.

The problems of the present and the risks of the future are deep and plain. But let it not be said that this generation refused to give up so little in order to achieve so much.

—R.N.

Part Two

1 STUDENT ACTIVISM: THE PAST—THE POTENTIAL

In many ways the campus of 1970-71 was strangely reminiscent of the aloof academia of the 1950's—a time when schools were closed worlds, hermetically sealed from surrounding social concerns; when students went to class, earned diplomas, and resolutely marched off to the suburbs; when a student rebel was someone who refused to wear white bucks and an activist was a person who could drink two beers at the same time.

There were obvious changes: differences in the style of dress, beards instead of crew cuts, and grass instead of beer. But the similarities in student response to social concerns could not be ignored. If graduates were not marching off to corporate offices with the same élan as their counterparts in the 1950's, they were drifting off into an equally remote world of communes and retreats in the woods. The meetings, rallies, and protests that had stirred the campus during the 1960's were submerged. In their place was a general willingness among students to forget protest, ignore the outside world, and return to the ivory

isolation of their classrooms or their personal utopias.
The civil rights movement, the antiwar movement, and
the battle for student rights seemed to have left mostly
disillusionment and despair.

But if the lessons learned in the student movement of
the 1960's were bitter, they were nonetheless instructive.
They showed that students have enormous resources at
their disposal, that they have the potential for providing
the direction, the manpower, the energy, and the ideals
to make an impact on the rest of society. In the 1960's
students led the way onto the freedom buses. They were
among the first to recognize the horrors of the Vietnam
War. Earth Day and its sequels centered on the nation's
campuses. Today, no less than then, students can give
direction to the country. Students of the 1970's inherit
this potential as well as the disillusionment of their col-
lective past. But they have not yet decided what to do
with either.

The Problem of Continuity

The apathy and discouragement apparent among
many students today is only partly due to their frustration with the system and its meager response to their
most vigorous efforts. They are also frustrated by the
facts of student life that mitigate against continuity,
make it difficult to organize across numerous campuses,
and hinder long-range efforts that can carry through
with the expectations raised on initiating a program
for reform. All student activities, whether academic,

political, athletic, or extra-curricular, suffer from a lack of continuity. Other groups suffer from the same problem, but with students it is especially severe. Their stay on campus is punctuated by summer vacations, mid-term holidays, exams, papers, and concern with career plans. Seldom are they able to apply all of their efforts to the solution of a particular problem. Thus, student activism tends to be a sporadic response to a crisis situation, often followed by frustration and depression from lack of success.

Students' inability to follow through on a project is most serious is social welfare areas. If projects dealing with people's lives and well-being are dropped in midstream, the consequences are serious. For example, if a ghetto literacy program is discontinued because of summer vacation, people suffer more than if the second annual dance never occurs. In the early 1960's civil rights workers filled the South during vacation period. Projects were started and expectations rose. But in September when the school bell rang, a mass exodus occured. Students returned to their classrooms, taking experiences with them, but leaving the problems and their solutions far behind.

The campus peace movement has suffered from the same discontinuities. Its yearly progression can be charted on a graph. Activism rises in the fall after details like housing and registration are taken care of, and peaks in mid-November before winter arrives. During December, January, and February activist blood thickens and slows, and a kind of hibernation occurs. The first warm day in

March rekindles fervor, and activism is again the fashion
until May and the approach of final exams. Summer
vacation occasions another three-month lull, and in the
fall the whole cycle begins anew. If this description
sounds cynical, try to remember a January peace march
or a major August demonstration. They are as rare as
Pentagon doves.

Unfortunately, social problems rarely adapt themselves
to student schedules. The urban ghetto still suffers when
students are on vacation. Price fixing, sex discrimination,
and deceptive packaging do not cease during exam periods. Even though Earth Day 1970 raised the level of
public concern about the quality of the environment, it
did not clean the air, strain sewage from rivers, or alle-
viate other environmental problems. A continuous, focused effort is required even to dent the surface of these
problems.

The same situation prevails in the political world. In
May 1970 thousands of students journeyed to Washington to protest the Cambodian invasion. But in August
when the McGovern-Hatfield Amendment to end the war
came to a vote, the halls of Congress were empty of students. The vote didn't fit into the student activist timetable.

A New Student Activism

Some students are beginning to realize that the old
strategies and structures of the student movement must be
altered to meet new realities. Though the ideals may re-

main the same, the problems do not. For example, equal opportunity today no longer involves the small Southern motel or movie theatre. It centers on the corporation—distant, highly anonymous, powerful far beyond a cadre of small-town police or angry citizens. The problems today involve more subtle violations of human rights than those which were fought in the past decade—violations of a worker's right to health and safety on the job, a community's right to a clean environment, and a citizen's right to participate in decisions that affect him.

Problems that absorbed students in the 1960's tended to be visible, localized, and susceptible to solutions by direct citizen action. Abuses today tend to be hidden. Discrimination is no longer advertised by a "whites only" sign at a lunch counter. It is often revealed only by painstaking documentation of corporate hiring practices, by searches of government files, or by sophisticated analyses of college board exams. Solutions are also more complex, requiring knowledge of law, economics, and, in the case of environmental abuse, science and engineering.

Take for example the corporate polluter. Sit-ins and marches will not clean up the rivers and the air that he fouls. He is too powerful and there are too many like him. Yet the student has unique access to the resources that can be effective in confronting the polluter. University and college campuses have the means for detecting the precise nature of the industrial effluent, through chemical or biological research. Through research such as they perform every day in the classroom, students can show the effect of the effluent on an entire watershed, and thus alert the community to real and demonstrable dangers to public health—a far more powerful way to arouse public support for a clean environment than a sit-in. Using the expertise of the campus, students can also demonstrate the technological means available for abating the discharge, and thus meet the polluter's argument that he can do nothing to control his pollution. By drawing on the knowledge of economists, students can counter arguments that an industry will go bankrupt or close down if forced to install pollution controls. Law and political science students can investigate the local, state, or Federal regulations that may apply to the case, and publicly challenge the responsible agencies to fulfill their legal duties.

Utilizing a variety of disciplines, students can fashion powerful investigative teams to affect an array of problems facing their society. They can study, for example, the economic incentives for community waste recycling, analyze overpackaging, and investigate methods of solid waste disposal—a far more effective and sophisticated approach to the solid waste problem than the more frequent litter cleanup campaign.

Instead of simply decrying race or sex discrimination in employment, students can use surveys, questionnaires, and job interviews to gather hard evidence of discrimination where it exists. Such evidence can serve as the basis for a formal complaint to the Equal Employment Opportunities Commission and for a suit under Title VII of the Civil Rights Act of 1964.

Evidence of price fixing is available in hundreds of government files to the persevering investigator. In the areas of both employment discrimination and price fixing, courts reward successful complainants payment either of attorney's fees, back wages, or damage awards. This is a tangible result that is entirely within the grasp of students.

In the past, student researchers have compiled an impressive record in many areas. A student investigation followed by a critical report precipitated the transformation of the moribund Federal Trade Commission into a more vigorous consumer-oriented agency. Voting drives spearheaded by seventeen and eighteen year olds produced the 26th Amendment of the United States Constitution. A graduate student at the University of Western Ontario, Norvald Fimreite, was the first to report mercury residues in fish caught in the Great Lakes and thereby unleash a nationwide alert on the problems of this deadly chemical in fish.

These approaches are far removed from the older tactics of the student movement, which centered on mass demonstrations, highly publicized confrontations with authorities, and summer projects such as the Mississippi voter registration drives and freedom marches. The new problems require more expertise, lengthy and often arduous research, and tedious interviews with minor bureaucrats. As yet, this prescription for action has found all too few adherents on the campus. Successful FTC investigations and voting drives are the exception rather than the rule. Few students have been willing to exchange the easy paths of sloganeering or indifference for lonely hours in the library and inglorious confrontations with low-level officials. But it is to be remembered that, at least as far as world society and ecology are concerned, the young — the students — will inherit the earth. In a very real sense, it is up to them to prod and to provoke, to research and to act, to assure that something remains worth inheriting.

The Student Public Interest Research Group

Unless continuity, expertise, and direction are joined together, there is little hope that students can bring about social betterment. Unless the cycles of vacation and classes, of home life and campus living, and of rising and falling activity can be eliminated, student movements are doomed to partial success at best. Stagnation is likely to occur if the same stale tactics continue. If things are to get done, a new approach is desperately needed.

Students now need the help of professionals in their social efforts. Professionals can bring not only their expertise — for example, their credentials to practice law in a court — but also the continuity of full-time work on the problems. A coalition of students and professionals can provide a workable vehicle for students to pursue their ideals and apply their talents. At the same time, professionals — lawyers, economists, scientists, and engineers — can provide the direction and staying power, as well as the specialized knowledge that is required.

This is the theory behind a student Public Interest Research Group (PIRG). There is no reason that students cannot hire a full-time professional staff to act as the backbone of their social consciences. With a minimal contribution from each student on a campus, they will have the resources to set up an ongoing organization that will remain stable as student bodies change. Through elected representatives, students from campuses across a state can join in concerted action on problems that concern them.

The idea of students hiring a full-time professional staff to carry out projects is not new. Universities themselves began when groups of students with common interests hired tutors. Later, tutors and students joined together to hire administrators to provide support. Today free schools are being developed at which students hire teachers to aid them in learning. More recently, student government officers have hired professionals to run student union buildings and to provide athletic and cultural services on campus. In California, Texas, and other states, students have hired lobbyists and lawyers to represent them before the legislature and the courts. The logical extension is that students should hire a full-time staff to help them work on issues affecting consumers, the environment, and other public problems.

Special interest groups like trade associations, professional associations, unions, and education associations already hire professional advocates to represent their vested economic interests. Decision-makers in government too frequently are cut off from all influences save those exerted by these special interest groups. Public interest advocates hired by students would provide a needed voice for unrepresented public interests. They would also open the doors of government to ordinary citizens who usually do not have the time or talent to find their way through complex public agencies.

Student investigators working with professionals can begin to probe deeply into the activities of city and state administrative agencies to ascertain whether they are carrying out their legislative mandates. They can scrutinize the marketplace for evidence of unfair trade practices. They can examine factory conditions to uncover occupational health or safety hazards. They can study taxation systems to determine equitability. They can act as monitors to guard against discrimination on grounds of race, sex, or creed. Finally, they will stand ready to act in new areas affecting the general public as those areas emerge.

2 THE MEANS

The notion of students and professionals combining their energy and expertise to solve social problems may at first seem uncomplicated and straightforward. But questions of how to mobilize this team immediately arise.

The first decision to be made is the size of the student constituency. Should students from only one campus band together? From several? Should the group be regional, statewide, or wider still? A number of considerations indicate that statewide or regional organizations of students and professionals is best.

1. To create an effective PIRG, with a staff of ten or more professionals, requires the support of at least seventy thousand students if the financial demands of the organization are to be met (see model budget at the end of this chapter). Few university campuses are so large; and, given the possibility that some students will not join in paying for the PIRG, a student constituency should be larger than seventy thousand. Except in rare cases, a single-campus PIRG is undesirable. Don't for-

get, too, that a PIRG at a single campus is unlikely to command either the financial resources of a larger group or the attention of the press and the support of state and local government that are essential if the PIRG's work is to be of any value.

2. The states, unlike municipalities and counties, are *sovereign units of government*, subject only to the Federal and state Constitutions. Thus the legal and political actions of a PIRG are most suitably directed either to the states or to the Federal government itself, since in these governments power resides. Even in those cases where a PIRG would most practicably be organized regionally (see point 4 below), the PIRG should maintain an office in the state capital.

3. It is always possible to combine the activities of two or more PIRGs when the issues involved require it. For example, a study of pollution in Lake Michigan might require the combined efforts of PIRGs in Michigan, Indiana, Illinois, and Wisconsin, and in such a case joint efforts can be made. But combining the state PIRGs administratively would limit their scope of activity: why would students in Michigan, for instance, want to spend their time and money investigating sex discrimination in Peoria, Illinois?

4. In most cases, students within a state share a community of interest that may not be found in other configurations of the PIRG. Most students in public universities—by far the largest group of students in the nation— are citizens of the state they study in. In some states,

however, statewide organization would be impractably cumbersome. There are, for example, some seven hundred thousand students in the California community colleges alone, plus hundreds of thousands more in state and private colleges and universities. Moreover, the size and diversity of California, like Texas and New York, suggests that regional PIRGs would be best: Northern and Southern California, New York City/ Long Island and Upstate New York, and so on.

Second, if lack of continuity was one of the chief weaknesses of previous student efforts, it also remains the major obstacle to student-supported Public Interest Research Groups. To attract a professional staff and embark on major research projects, one must guarantee a certain amount of stability and continuity. Without some measure of certainty about next month's pay check, few professionals would be willing to risk jobs and careers to work with students. It is psychologically difficult, if not impossible, to begin work on a two-year investigation without a strong likelihood of being able to complete it.

The key to continuity is a stable financial base. Without an orderly, relatively secure funding system, continuity is impossible. There is no escaping this fact. So it is necessary to decide at the outset what funding system will work best, and how to implement it.

Funding Systems

Sporadic and uneven contributions from dances, solicitations, or cafeteria contributions a la the March of

Dimes can contribute money to a Public Interest Research Group, but they are not suitable as sole or even primary sources of revenue. In the first place, all these devices are gambles; one cannot predict their success. How many professionals would want to gamble their salary on the outcome of a concert or a door-to-door solicitation? Second, even if these promotions were successful, they would not supply enough money to support a professional staff. Third, each requires a vast, wasteful expenditure of time, energy, and money. Instead of obtaining educational benefits by performing substantive research, students would be continually forced to devise ways of raising money.

Rather than launch a campaign which operates at a serious disadvantage from the outset, why not utilize the normal fee-collecting processes of the university to raise funds? At most schools, students pay an incidental fee, in addition to or as part of their tuition. This money goes to support athletics, extracurricular activities, health services, and other similar activities. Normally, all fees are mandatory, though sometimes a special fee, such as insurance, is optional and has to be signed up for specially.

THE CHECKOFF SYSTEM

A checkoff system (*i.e.,* checking a card at registration) is not a viable alternative for a Public Interest Research Group. In essence, it is no different from a voluntary donation which offers no predictability or continuity. Moreover, it forces students to decide whether or not they want to support the plan before they have the information to make an intelligent decision. It puts incoming freshmen and transfer students in a particularly bad position. Besides, the increased expense of processing an additional card in the registration packet would be prohibitive. Most universities charge fifteen to twenty cents for processing each registration card. In the case of a PIRG, if a dollar fee were involved, the cost would come to 15-20 per cent of the total amount collected. Such a cost is both exhorbitant and unnecessary.

THE MANDATORY FEE SYSTEM

Mandatory fees eliminate the need for fund-raising campaigns and provide a stable financial base. In the past, students rarely have been consulted as to whether their fees should be increased, reduced, or discontinued. Recent attempts to divert thousands of dollars now spent for football to minority scholarships or other social welfare programs have met with no success. Thus, although the mandatory fee guarantees funding, it is shamelessly coercive. The university offers its students two choices: pay or leave. Nothing lies between.

THE VOLUNTARY FEE INCREASE WITH A GUARANTEED REFUND PROVISION

The mandatory fee system is less coercive when students are given a choice to determine initially whether they wish to increase their fees to support a new activity.

It is then essentially a voluntary fee. The last element of coercion is removed when all students who do not want to support an activity, even if it is approved by a majority, are refunded that portion of their fee payment.

Although this kind of fee payment is not as certain a source of funds as a mandatory fee without a refund, it is, nevertheless, capable of supporting a Public Interest Research Group.

The voluntary system which includes a guaranteed refund operates in the following way. First, a majority of all students indicate by ballot or petition that they want to start a Public Interest Research Group and fund it by a fee increase. Second, the organizers must seek approval for the increase from the appropriate administrative board. Third, if approved, the collection plan, with its refund provision, is implemented.

The majority of the student body should have the right to determine the procedures for collecting the money so long as the minority is guaranteed the right to obtain a refund. The best way to insure the rights of the dissenting minority is to make all refunds from the registrar's office or another convenient location on campus. Refunding should occur the third or fourth week after each registration period. By setting up a standard procedure, students will know exactly when and where to collect their refunds, and administrative costs are minimized. This also allows the organizers to determine the amount of money available to the PIRG at a specific time.

The three-week lapse between the registration period

and the refund time permits all students, especially freshmen and transfers, to find out about the group and decide whether they want to support it. In addition, it allows the administrative staff of the university time to
clear its desks of the paperwork of registration.

The funding mechanism is predicated on obtaining
majority approval from the student body and the sub-
sequent right of the majority to establish an equitable
funding system. Without this approval, the fee increase
cannot be called voluntary, and there is no difference
between it and any other mandatory fee. There are two
basic ways a student body can approve PIRG funding:
petition or referendum.

Petition or Referendum?

The referendum is probably not the best way of obtaining student approval for a PIRG. Past experience
shows that fewer than 50 percent of the eligible voters
participate in a campus referendum even when the issue
to be voted on is hotly debated and of great interest to
most students. As a practical matter, it is almost impossible to obtain approval from a majority of the student
body (not just those voting) in a referendum. This is
especially true in large universities. A petition campaign
then is the best means of obtaining decisive support for
a PIRG.

A petition campaign safeguards student rights in several ways. A handful of glib students with access to
printing facilities can publicize and promote a referen-

dum. But to organize a successful petition drive, hundreds of workers are needed, thus helping to assure that support for the program is widespread. Another benefit of the petition campaign is the opportunity it gives students to engage in a dialogue with the petitioner. This almost guarantees that the plan is understood fully. The effort required to reach out and educate a majority of the student body will insure that all students, faculty members, administrators, regents, and trustees are apprised of the plan.

The Fee Increase

The amount of the fee increase should not be so large as to constitute a burden on poorer students. Most schools which have approved the plan so far have increased fees by $1.00 per student per quarter or $1.50 per student per semester. This sum amounts to a fee increase for the individual student of *less than a penny per day*.

For the vast majority of students this amount of money is so trivial as to pass unnoticed. In 1969, the average college student in the United States spent close to $250.00 per year on liquor, soft drinks, beer, and cigarettes. Surely $3.00 to help battle job discrimination, pollution, or consumer fraud is not too much.

Although each individual contribution is minimal, the aggregate is large enough to fund a Public Interest Research Group. For example, if 71,000 students from 10 schools participate in the plan and pay $1.50 per semester $213,000.00 would be collected. Considering the operating costs of a PIRG, this sum is not unreasonably large. Salaries for the professionals, equipment, and student wages are costly expenses. If fewer students participate, the group can be scaled down accordingly.

The budget on the following pages illustrates the major expenses.

PIRG: A MODEL BUDGET

(Estimated operating expenses for one fiscal year for a PIRG with support base of between seventy thousand and eighty thousand students. This model may be expanded or reduced to fit different size student bases.)

A. EMPLOYEE COSTS

10 Professionals (for example, 9 professionals—$9,500.00; 1 executive director—$13,500.00) $ 99,000.00

4 Secretarial and clerical employees (for example, 1 administrative secretary—$650.00 per month; 2 secretaries—$500.00 per month)   19,800.00

2 Full-time equivalent community workers—$6,000 each   12,000.00

     $ 130,800.00

Employee benefits   14,700.00

Total Employee Costs $ 145,500.00

B. OCCUPANCY COSTS

Space rental (2,100 sq. ft. at $4.50 per sq. ft. per year) $ 9,450.00

Electricity—$40.00 per month   480.00

Total Occupancy Costs $ 9,930.00

C. OFFICE EQUIPMENT

4 Electric typewriters—$390.00 each $ 1,560.00

14 Desks and chairs (for example, 10 desks and swivel armchairs at $210.00 each; 4 secretarial desks and chairs at $240.00 each)   3,060.00

24 Side chairs—$30.00 each   720.00

8 File cabinets—4-drawer

3 legal-size—$95.00 each   285.00

5 letter-size—$85.00 each   425.00

10 Book shelves—$95.00 each   950.00

Total Equipment Costs	$	7,000.00
Equipment cost amortized over 10 years	$	700.00
Typewriter maintenance—$42.00 per machine		168.00
Total Equipment Cost per year	$	868.00

D. CONTINGENCY FUND
Includes cost of books and legal publications, projected litigation costs
$ 7,500.00

E. OFFICE COSTS
Consumable supplies—$200.00 per person X 14 $ 2,800.00
Telephone:
Key-type switchboard—$250.00 per month (5 lines plus intercom)   3,000.00
Long-distance calls—$7.50 per day X 240   1,800.00
Postage—40 mailings per day X 240   768.00
Duplicating costs—$100.00 per month (machine rental and use)   1,200.00
Total Office Costs $ 9,558.00

F. STUDENT RESEARCH PROJECTS
For example, 15–20 summer projects, grants of approximately $1,000.00 each, to cover equipment, operating expenses, and minimal wages.
$ 20,000.00

G. PUBLIC EDUCATION
Includes cost of publishing PIRG reports, advertising, and other publicity
$ 12,000.00

H. CERTIFIED PUBLIC ACCOUNTANT
Annual audit of PIRG financial records
$ 500.00

TOTAL ANNUAL OPERATING EXPENSES $ 205,866.00

3 THE STRUCTURE
OF THE PUBLIC INTEREST
RESEARCH GROUP

The vague notion of a PIRG advocating student concerns must be translated into the realities of a functioning organization composed of a dozen or more schools and fifty thousand to one hundred thousand students. Student PIRG organizations cannot leave to chance the spirit of interschool cooperation that will unite all or most campuses of a state into a functioning body. They must build the intercampus relationship into the structure of the organization before the plan is publicized or student approval sought. They must clearly delineate lines of authority and control to insure fair representation and avoid needless misunderstanding and antagonism. Obviously, no final plan can be adopted until all participating schools have passed the proposal and elected student boards of directors. But a clear idea of organization should be formulated at the outset.

The precise form of the organization may vary from group to group but the following model should apply in most cases.

Overview

On each campus where the PIRG concept receives student and administrative approval, students elect representatives for local boards of directors. In turn, each local board selects one or more of its members to represent it on a state board. The state board consists of local board representatives from all participating colleges and universities.

The large number of students involved and the geographical diversity of participating schools necessitate this hierarchical structure* for student representation. There is no practical way for tens of thousands of students, separated by hundreds of miles, to vote individually on each proposed activity of the group. Nor is it possible for any meaningful communication to occur between the professional staff and such large numbers of students, except through representative boards.

Even to include all local board members on a state board is unfeasible. In Minnesota, for example, over one hundred students serve on local boards at eighteen participating universities. Such a large group meeting once or twice a month would be prohibitively expensive and logistically impossible.

The Local Boards

Depending on the size of the university and its past

*See Table I.

TABLE I

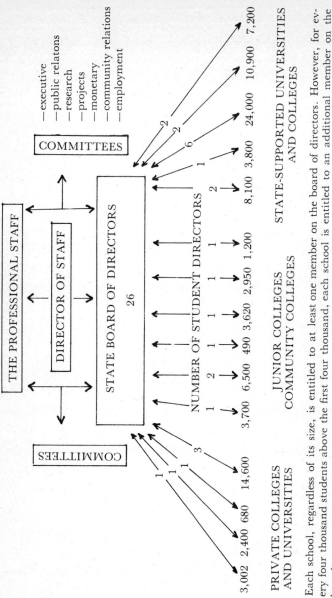

THE PROFESSIONAL STAFF

DIRECTOR OF STAFF

STATE BOARD OF DIRECTORS
26

COMMITTEES

—executive
—public relatons
—research
—projects
—monetary
—community relations
—employment

NUMBER OF STUDENT DIRECTORS

STATE-SUPPORTED UNIVERSITIES
AND COLLEGES

2 2 6 1 2
7,200 10,900 24,000 3,800 8,100

JUNIOR COLLEGES
COMMUNITY COLLEGES

1 1 1 1 2 1
1,200 2,950 3,620 490 6,500 3,700

PRIVATE COLLEGES
AND UNIVERSITIES

3 1 1 1
14,600 680 2,400 3,002

Each school, regardless of its size, is entitled to at least one member on the board of directors. However, for every four thousand students above the first four thousand, each school is entitled to an additional member on the board.

traditions, elections of local boards may be held on a campuswide or school-by-school basis. The size of the university usually will determine the number of representatives selected.

The principal duty of the local board is to represent the interests of its constituents to the state board. It serves as a clearinghouse for complaints and suggestions; it carries out preliminary investigations; and it proposes worthwhile projects to the state board for consideration. At regular public meetings of the local board, students, faculty, and members of the community can present proposals and hear reports on the activities of the professional staff.

The local board may undertake projects on its own, and mobilize campus resources to carry out projects suggested by the state board and the professional staff. To avoid duplication of effort, however, the local board should coordinate all projects with the ongoing work of campus and community groups. To do this effectively, the local board must develop ties with student, faculty, and community groups. Creation of a board of advisors may make this job easier. In addition to these activities, the local board is responsible for disbursing refunds after each registration period.

The State Board

Each local board elects representatives to the state board from among its own members. Every university gets at least one seat, with additional seats distributed on a proportionate basis. For example, in Minnesota, for every five thousand students above an initial five thousand, schools receive an additional seat on the state board. Thus, with eighteen hundred students, Carleton College has one seat, Mankato State College with twelve thousand students has two seats, and the Minneapolis campus of the University of Minnesota, with forty-one thousand five hundred students, has eight state board seats.

The primary duty of the state board is to select priority areas from the mass of projects that may be presented. In general, the student board will determine overall strategy, leaving tactical decisions up to the professional staff. To pursue an effective strategy and maintain contact with the professional staff, the state board may elect an executive committee to act in interim periods between meetings. This committee is responsible to the state board for all its decisions. The state board must coordinate local board activities and insure proper use of the PIRG name and resources. It also coordinates activities with other state public interest organizations and, if useful, initiates joint projects. For example, the Minnesota group (MPIRG) might become the northernmost link in a multistate project focusing on the improvement of water quality in the Mississippi River.

Although the state board has authority over the professional staff and can order it to undertake or discontinue work on a project, the board must not exercise this power indiscreetly. Lawyers and scientists will not work for a student group if its actions prove to be arbitrary and capricious. The need for student control must balance against the professionals' need for independence and freedom of action on a day-to-day basis.

The Professional Staff

The professional staff is the action arm of the student PIRG. It consists of lawyers, scientists, and other professionals, hired by the state board. One member of the professional staff, the director, is responsible to the board for the staff's activities. To insure the most efficient use of the professionals' time, individual staff members do not ordinarily work directly with members of the board. However, the board retains the option to consult directly with members of the staff when necessary.

Because the staff consists of professionals with expertise in a variety of subject areas, there are many possibilities for action and many forms that action can take. Obviously the first step in any project is research. Depending on the project, this may be undertaken by a member of the professional staff, by student research groups, by student-faculty groups (in some cases it might be appropriate to make research part of a regular course or seminar), or by other task forces. On the basis of this research the professional staff recommends action to the state board.

If the recommendation is approved, the staff director assigns a professional to proceed with the project. The gravity and urgency of the problem determines the appropriate response. Ordinarily, the staff pursues a gradually escalating series of tactics. Fact-finding, persuasion, public education, and lobbying usually precede litigation.*

The Legal Structure

The PIRG should be set up as a nonprofit, tax-exempt corporation. (See Chapter 7 for discussion about tax questions.) This corporation is a separate legal entity, distinct from each of the participating schools. Students elect a student board of directors, and the board appoints

---

TABLE II
OUTLINE OF PIRG STRUCTURE

Duties of the Local Board
1. Serve as a link between students and the state board.
2. Mobilize campus resources to work on projects organized by the professional staff.
3. Supervise projects of its own design.
4. Cooperate with other campus and community groups.
5. Elect and, if necessary, recall representatives to the state board.

Duties of the State Board
1. Determine priority areas for professional staff action.
2. Supervise the activities of the local boards.
3. Coordinate PIRG projects with other state or national public interest groups.
4. Assume responsibility for all financial and administrative details pertaining to the professional staff.
5. Serve as the official spokesman of the group.

Activities of the Professional Staff
1. Implement the decisions of the state board.
2. Supervise student/faculty research teams.
3. Engage in research, investigations, public education, lobbying, and litigation.

---

*See Table II.

or elects the officers of the corporation. These officers are usually members of the student board.

The corporation has to establish binding legal contracts with participating schools setting forth the rights and obligations of each. In general, the contract is not very different from that signed by the food services corporation or any other entity that does business with the university. The food services corporation agrees to provide so many meals per day, per week, or per month in consideration for use of university kitchens and a certain sum of money. The PIRG similarly agrees to do (and not to do) certain activities in consideration for the fee per student per quarter. Likewise, the university agrees to serve as a collecting agent for the PIRG. Both the university and the PIRG have the legal right to enforce their contract.

4 THE HISTORY OF THE FIRST STUDENT PIRGS

The preceding outline of PIRG expenses, function, and organization is based on experience with student groups in several states. The original idea for student Public Interest Research Groups grew out of the work of Ralph Nader and his staff during the summer and fall of 1970. The essence of their proposal was that students tax themselves a nominal sum in order to hire a group of lawyers, scientists, engineers, and other professionals to seek solutions to public interest problems.

The need for new public interest professionals had become increasingly apparent during the preceding year. The handful of Washington public interest lawyers and scientists did not have the resources and, in some cases, the range of expertise, to deal with complicated local issues. Consequently, many battles were lost by default.

At the same time hundreds of graduates of law and medical schools were seeking but not finding employment in the private public-service area. The chief obstacle they encountered was lack of funds. Given the magnitude of the problems facing the country it was imperative that 20

percent or more of the best graduates in the nation begin working for public interest causes. The graduates
were willing even though salaries and prestige often were
low. However, there were job openings for fewer than
one-tenth of one percent of these committed men and
women. Therefore one important impetus behind the plan
was the desire to increase opportunities for public interest
employment so as not to waste the idealism and energy
of these young professionals.

During the course of the summer various kinds of new
public interest firms were studied. The first suggestion
examined was a firm capable of harnessing the part-
time talents of professionals associated with private law
firms or industry. It was felt that these women and men
could best be used to supplement and back up the efforts
of a full-time staff. However, because of conflicting obligations they could not handle certain types of cases, nor
would part-time volunteers entirely supplant full-time
workers. Volunteers are too unstable a base on which to
build a far-reaching institution-changing public interest
group.

A second model examined involved the use of law,
medical, and science students. Their work would be
integrated into their regular clinical curricula. However,
this type of firm would marshal limited expertise and
provide no continuity. Like the assistance of part-time
volunteers, the work of students would be a welcome
addition to the efforts of the regular staff, but neither
could replace the full-time staff.

The only proposal which seemed to answer all expec-

tations was to form on the local level the same type of
groups that already existed in Washington, D.C. Unfortunately, the reality of the situation was that the
Washington firms themselves were already extended to
their limits and had neither the manpower nor the
finances to establish local affiliates. Foundations could
provide enough money to start only a handful of demonstration firms and most foundations were already
fully committed. Besides, foundation money almost always has a two- or three-year time limit. At the end of
that period new sources of support must be located. A
few years will not be long enough to bring about struc-
tural change.

Only a very few private individuals are willing or
able to turn $150,000 over to as novel an organization
as a public interest firm. Most who have the resources
donate their money to a school, church, or hospital. Why
chance controversy when so many other worthwhile
charities exist?

In a few large cities public interest firms can support
themselves by charging fees, but most by necessity are
small in size and their work is mostly limited to clients
who can afford to pay or cases which can produce fees.
Rather than depend on the short-term contributions of
foundations and philanthropists, it was decided to form
groups of professionals with a wider and more permanent financial base.

Students seemed an obvious choice to fill this prescription. In the first place they were among the most

severe critics of present-day society, and, second, they could provide a great deal more than funding. The campuses could be turned into huge public interest centers and the part-time efforts of students could provide a strong backup to the work of the full-time staff. For these and other reasons it was decided to entrust the PIRG proposal to students.

During September and October 1970 Nader and four of his associates visited over 40 campuses proposing the plan. By the end of the academic year, students in many states across the country had responded, and the first two student-supported Public Interest Research Groups were formed in Oregon and Minnesota. Students in West Virginia, Utah, Washington, Georgia, Hawaii, Illinois, Massachusetts, and Missouri began plans to establish groups in their respective states.

Students in Oregon responded first. The idea spread quickly to many campuses in the state. Interested students formed steering committees and began planning the Oregon Student Public Interest Research Group (OSPIRG). By January, every school in the State System of Higher Education, four private schools, and four out of twelve community colleges had obtained signatures from over 50 percent of their student bodies. At most schools, OSPIRG received more support than any other issue in the school's history.

By early December, students at the Minneapolis/St. Paul campuses of the University of Minnesota were planning a similar petition campaign. As in Oregon, the idea spread rapidly to other schools in the state. Organizations came to life on many campuses, and the effort to establish the Minnesota Public Interest Research Group (MPIRG) became a reality. In late January, MPIRG held a statewide petition drive. The University of Minnesota obtained signatures of support from more than 60 percent of its fifty-three-thousand member student body in less than two weeks. Other state-supported and private universities followed close behind, registering equally impressive backing. By the end of the spring quarter, over fifty thousand signatures from students on eighteen campuses throughout the state had been collected.

After obtaining these overwhelming demonstrations of student support, the long process of negotiation with college administrations and appropriate boards of education began. In Oregon, the State Board of Higher Education raised the issue of mandatory fee collection and the propriety of using such fees for the proposed purposes. The Board's apprehensions centered on a feeling that OSPIRG might "adversely politicize the neutrality of higher education." The element which troubled the Board most was the provision for litigation in the OSPIRG program. After many hours of dialogue, the Board agreed to sanction the collection of a mandatory fee with a refund provision but temporarily withheld support for the litigation function.

In Minnesota, there are three systems of higher education: the university system, the state four-year and junior colleges, and the private schools. In all discussions the issue of mandatory fee collection received considerable scrutiny. After hours of negotiation and in the light of legislative support, the Board of Regents of the University of Minnesota and the boards of trustees of several private colleges accepted the MPIRG proposal. As in Oregon, the proposal called for a fee increase of $1.00 per student per quarter (or $1.50 per student per semester) to be collected by the school during the regular registration periods. In both cases the right for the dissenting student to obtain a full refund was provided. To insure participation of state and junior colleges, MPIRG received legislative support for the collection of a mandatory fee. Approval now seems certain for the state and junior colleges to join MPIRG.

Upon approval in both states, MPIRG and OSPIRG held the first elections for their respective boards of directors. The groups have now begun selection of the professional staffs. Applications from lawyers, scientists, and college professors have poured into both state offices.

The development of statewide student PIRGs provides an unusually good opportunity for lawyers, scientists, engineers, political scientists, social workers, and other professionals to become advocates for the public interest. Eventually, as the idea spreads, it will offer a new career category in public service: the independent public interest professional.

5 HOW TO ORGANIZE

The techniques used to build support for a Public Interest Research Group will vary depending on the size, diversity, and type of school. Small, homogeneous colleges require less effort to build support than large universities which have sizable numbers of commuters and graduate and professional students. Advice and assistance on organizing a PIRG is available from the Washington, D.C., PIRG (see Appendix for address).

The organizing effort usually begins with a small group of interested students on each campus willing to spend long hours planning, discussing, and proselytizing.* For example, in Minnesota a group of fifteen students worked five months before gaining widespread support. At the same time, students on the other campuses should be contacted and the concept spread to every school in the state. Representatives from each school should meet with their counterparts at a series of state meetings.

*See chart of Model Timetable.

Save as before.

The strength or weakness of the core group is decisive. The core group should include students from all segments of the campus. While it may be self-gratifying to think that a handful of students from a single dormitory can form a PIRG, it is also an illusion. Unless all segments of the student community are involved in the effort, the idea will not succeed.

Various campus groups initially may feel threatened by "another new group" seeking student support. Unwarranted animosity can be avoided by opening the avenues for cooperation at the outset and making clear the aims and objectives of the Public Interest Research Group. If the plan is presented correctly, student governments, women's groups, and minority groups will support the organizing effort. Each has an interest in creating a strong action-oriented organization to pursue public interest causes.

The organizing group must perform three distinct but related tasks: fund raising, publicity, and petitioning.

Fund Raising

Every campaign requires money to pay for posters, leaflets, and office expenses. The total cost of the Oregon campaign, involving fourteen schools and about seventy-five thousand students, amounted to seven thousand dollars over a six-month period. In Minnesota, the campaign cost less than five thousand dollars, even though it involved seventeen schools and almost one hundred thousand students. Presumably, the costs

---

MODEL TIMETABLE

1st Week Introduction of the student PIRG plan to students on various campuses throughout the state or region. At the end of the first week, state or regional meeting to bring schools together to discuss the need for a PIRG, the necessity for unity, and the strategy for the statewide or regional effort.

2nd Week Explanation of the PIRG plan to students on all campuses by news articles and other media. Development of core groups on each campus not contacted during the first week.

3rd Week Second state or regional meeting. Initial phase of outlining specific PIRG model and proposal. Drafting of petition and design of new publicity.

4th and 5th Weeks More intense effort to notify students of the effort under way. Low-key publicity campaign, intensifying and climaxing with accent on the upcoming petition campaign. Third state or regional meeting.

6th Week Petition drive.

7th and 8th Weeks Completion of petition drive with greater than 50 percent support in each school. Fourth state or regional meeting. Development of strategy to be used in approaching governing boards.

9th Week Beginning of negotiations for administration approval; the length of time negotiations last depends on who has to be negotiated with.

---

will continue to drop as organizing techniques are further refined.

The expense of the campaign can be minimized by obtaining donations of skills, facilities, and materials. Organizers should try to obtain access to free office space, a mimeograph machine, use of a school telephone, and access to low-cost printing supplies. In Minnesota and Oregon, students received donations of time and materials from carpenters, advertising agencies, lawyers, photographers, and other concerned citizens.

Money to fund the campaign may be available from

student governments or student unions. The student government at the University of Washington, for example, appropriated three thousand dollars to help the Washington state PIRG organize. In Oregon, individual students and faculty contributed four thousand dollars out of their own pockets. Students in western Massachusetts are using money received from an outside donor to help pay their expenses. In addition, the sale of bumper stickers, buttons, and silk-screen posters can raise funds.

Publicity

Students are not afflicted by the proclivity to give away money to a cause unless they understand and believe in it. The PIRG organizers must convey through their publicity campaign a sophisticated prescription for student action and motivate students to participate in the plan.

There are usually dozens of campus and community groups competing for student support. It is critical that the PIRG organizing effort stand out and avoid falling into the category of "just another group." The publicity campaign must convince students that Public Interest Research Groups signal an entirely new direction in the student movement and are worthy of support. It is important that the publicity campaign does not encourage students to sign petitions blindly, but rather that it makes students aware of the values and benefits of the PIRG plan.

From the outset, the group must determine the best

means to achieve maximum impact. Since the organizing effort may last for several months, the tempo of the publicity campaign must be carefully orchestrated. New posters and leaflets which can maintain the pace of the effort and hold attention should be prepared and displayed. A consistent theme in the posters and leaflets throughout the campaign may be helpful in establishing an identity for the PIRG organizing effort. In Oregon and Minnesota the slogans "Environmental Preservation," "Consumer Protection," and "Corporate Responsibility" were repeated again and again. The posters, buttons, and leaflets used in Minnesota were printed in combinations of green, black, and orange. The students soon identified these colors with the Minnesota PIRG. A graphic symbol appearing on material may also serve a similar purpose.

Discussion groups in dormitories, sororities and fraternities, as well as in student unions, give students an opportunity to find out the details of the plan and how they can become involved. In addition, any questions or objections they may have can be aired and resolved during these sessions.

The campus newspaper, radio, and television are invaluable sources of effective publicity. Very early in the effort, students should meet with representatives of each medium and explain the PIRG. The Washington, D.C., PIRG is willing to send to all campus media a free packet of background information and press clippings.

Local newspapers and television and radio stations

should be contacted, especially in commuter schools where students are linked more closely to the community. Plan to send out press releases on a regular basis and make every effort to gain editorial support. Besides the additional publicity the press can generate during the petitioning period, it is essential to contact newsmen because the eventual success of the PIRG will depend in large part on its ability to inform the public of the PIRG's actions and to influence public opinion.

Together with these traditional methods of publicity, more novel efforts are helpful in attracting student support. For example, at the University of Minnesota, students set up an elaborate multimedia presentation in the courtyard of the architecture building. An eight-minute filmstrip highlighted the effort. Giant green-and-orange banners silk-screened with the phrases "Environmental Quality," "Consumer Protection," and "Corporate Responsibility" were hung. Photographs, mobiles, and posters completed the display.

At Southern Illinois University, Buckminster Fuller's home campus, students constructed domes to advertise the Southern Illinois Public Interest Research Group.

At Oregon State University, students built a visual display depicting the effect of industrial sewage in a nearby river. The display was augmented by an explanation of how OSPIRG could solve the sewage problem by monitoring the industrial effluent and pressing for conformity to state and Federal water quality regulations.

The possibilities for such projects are limitless. The success or failure of the publicity campaign, however, should be measured less by its aesthetic impact than by its ability to provide students with a solid grasp of the goals and aims of the PIRG.

The Petition Drive

A petition drive to raise student fees will not be an easy task. Its success hinges on the efficacy of the publicity campaign and the ability of the petitioners to gain support on a one-to-one basis. The petitioners must strike a balance between oversell, which becomes obnoxious and counterproductive, and undersell, which becomes timid and ineffective. The petitioners must understand fully the concept of a Public Interest Research Group and be able to make clear the details of the plan.

The complete understanding of the petitioners cannot be left to chance. In both Oregon and Minnesota, petitioner booklets were prepared describing the rationale, structure, and goals of the group. The booklets were designed to give petitioners a working knowledge of the PIRG plan, plus additional hints on how to secure support. Lists of the most typical questions to be expected and their answers were included along with other information. Petitioners were asked to study the booklet and then attend a session at which members of the organizing committee answered questions and simulated petitioning situations.

Organization of the Petition Drive

The petition drive must be a well-coordinated effort in order to make the most efficient use of each petitioner's time. Before petitioning begins, establish when and where large groups of students can be found. In both Oregon and Minnesota, campuses were divided into three areas: university living areas, traffic centers, and classrooms.

UNIVERSITY LIVING AREAS

Dormitories, fraternities, sororities, and off-campus apartments are useful places to obtain support because they provide opportunities for individual and group contact. Make every effort to establish a liaison in each living group as early as possible. Frequently there are organized residence hall councils which can act as a source for these initial contacts.

It is advisable for students to petition within their own living groups, where they already have personal contacts. Students who live in dormitories frequently have a different perspective than students who live in Greek houses or off-campus. At Oregon State University, some dormitories had as many as three PIRG representatives on each floor. As a result, several dormitories registered 100 percent support.

TRAFFIC CENTERS

In large, predominantly commuter universities, petitioning in living units will not be enough. In order to contact students, identify the points on campus where many students congregate or pass through on their way to classes. These areas are the student traffic centers: student unions, libraries, heavily used walkways between buildings; in commuter campuses, student traffic centers also include bus stops, train stations, and parking areas.

In Oregon and Minnesota, organizers supplied each traffic center with either a table or a portable petition stand. A banner, visual display, or poster was set up to attract attention, and literature explaining the PIRG plan was made easily accessible. Be sure to take into consideration the times of day and the days of the week that students pass through these centers.

Students at Oregon State University and the University of Minnesota used on-the-spot reports and computer analyses to help determine the effectiveness of all centers. Every evening the petition information was tallied and a computer analysis run to gauge the results of each center.

CLASSROOMS

At the University of Minnesota, where more than 90 percent of the students are commuters, it was found that classroom buildings were heavily inhabited from nine A.M. to three P.M. The libraries were used most often in the evening between six P.M. and ten P.M. At the two largest universities in Oregon, many students live within walking distance of the campus. Though they were reluctant to sign petitions in the morning on their way to class, petitioners found students willing to sign on their way home.

Some traffic centers lose their effectiveness after a time because they are frequented by the same students. When petitioning success falls off in an area, the effort should be transferred to a new location. Failure to move can result in discouragement for petitioners and a crucial loss of potential signatures.

In both Oregon and Minnesota, petitioners were organized into teams responsible for a single traffic center. When the petition effort was moved, the group moved as a unit. This arrangement simplified scheduling and allowed the group to mold itself into a cohesive team. Petitioning was most effective when several students manned the petition center at once, and when they worked for two-hour periods.

For a thorough organizing effort, petition large lecture sections and seminar classes. Sympathetic professors may allow a student speaker five or ten minutes at the beginning of a class to explain the PIRG concept and enlist support. After a short explanation, pass out individual petition forms with space for only one signature. Individual petition forms allow petitioners to reach every student and minimize the use of class time. They also eliminate the confusion of trying to gather signatures as students rush in and out of class. Individual forms can also be used effectively to petition large crowds in auditoriums or at sporting events.

Petition Forms

The petition form is an important part of the overall campaign. It should be clear and concise. The following suggestions may be helpful.

1. Include a well-defined statement of purpose and a short explanation of the financial mechanism.

2. Provide a space for student names, addresses, and identification numbers so that signatures can be verified.

3. Number each petition form individually to facilitate record keeping and minimize the possibility of loss.

4. Record the petitioner's name and the numbers of the petitions he takes each time a new petition leaves the office.

5. Make each petitioner responsible for every petition checked out in his/her name. Do not leave petition forms unattended on tables or tacked up on walls. If a petition is lost, all of the signatures are lost with it.

Post-petitioning Letdown

During the petition drive, interest on campus reaches its peak. The campus newspaper headlines petition totals, local radio and television stations feature the organizing effort, and hundreds of students join the effort. The original core group expands rapidly. At the University of Minnesota, for example, Minneapolis/St. Paul media zeroed in on the campus during the two-week petition period and the organizing group multiplied from fifteen to four hundred.

Petition No._____

MODEL PETITION AND RESOLUTION

We, the undersigned, stand resolved that the_____Public Interest Research Group (_____PIRG) be established:

—The purpose of _____PIRG shall be to articulate and pursue through the media, the institutions of government, the courts, and other legal means the concerns of students on issues of general public interest.

—Issues will include environmental preservation, consumer protection, and the role of corporation and government agencies in the lives of the average citizen.

—_____PIRG shall be nonpartisan, nonprofit, and student controlled.

—It shall be financed by an increase in student fees of one dollar per student per quarter.

—Any student who does not wish to participate shall be entitled to a full refund during the third week of each quarter from an established public office of each campus.

We, students registered at the University of_____, hereby petition the Board of _____of the University of _____to authorize the formation of_____PIRG.

NAME	ADDRESS	STUDENT NO.
1.		
2.		
3.		
4.		
5.		
6.		
7.		

When the drive is completed and final tallies of the signatures are in, workers drift off to other activities, and the core group shrinks back to a few dozen of the most committed students. The intensity of the petition effort, coupled with neglected class work, is a prime reason for the fall-off.

The core group, of course, then turns its efforts to gain approval from the university and its governing board. As the proposal winds its way through various committees toward final approval, student spokesmen are required to attend dozens of meetings. If legislative approval is needed, a major lobbying effort may have to be undertaken. But this work is specialized and, for the most part, demands more commitment than the average student is prepared to make. Student research and action projects can be developed to maintain interest in the PIRG. Student researchers can gather data on environmental or consumer problems to provide a foundation for the work of the professional staff. Additionally, students can identify the agencies responsible for dealing with these problems.

With the help of interested faculty members, classes can be established to teach students the workings of the governmental system, the legal system in America, how a corporation operates, and how specific problems can be solved. Additional projects are outlined in Chapter 8.

6 GETTING UNDER WAY

Administrative Approval

After a successful petition campaign, students should establish a plan to secure approval from the appropriate board of education. The first step is to identify which board has the power to approve a fee increase. The administrative structure for higher education is different in every state, but in general private schools are governed by individual boards of trustees while state-supported institutions are controlled by regents or boards of education. Sometimes the power to increase fees in public schools is left to the state legislature, and to obtain a fee increase, new legislation is needed. A different situation occurs when the board has the power but refuses to exercise it without an indication of legislative support. If this is the case, individual legislators should be persuaded to indicate support by phone calls, letters, or telegrams. In many schools, the student senate or other student board has the power to raise fees. In this situation, the campaigners should bypass the administration and seek student approval directly.

It has been found that even overwhelming support expressed by the petition campaign does not guarantee approval from an administrative board. The board will examine closely each aspect of the proposal. One should anticipate a myriad of questions from board members and prepare answers to them before formally seeking approval. An indication of support for the PIRG proposal from government officials, community groups, and faculty members can also help persuade the board about the merits of the plan.

Support from national, state, and local officials should be sought. It is important, however, that this support be bipartisan to avoid implications of political alliance.

Because boards of education are usually attuned to the opinions of citizen groups, it is also important to seek community support. Too often in the past, students have unnecessarily alienated sectors of society, not because of what they said, but because of the way they said it. If the community feels a sense of identity with the PIRG, if it realizes that the PIRG's interests are its own, many traditional barriers can be broken down, and rapport can be established between students and community. Once the PIRG is approved, if it is to be successful, it has to influence public opinion, and all avenues of communication are essential.

If past experience is a true guide, one of the most important concerns of the administration will be the educational value of the PIRG. While it may seem obvious that all the activities of a PIRG have some educational value, and that many of the activities may be extraordinarily valuable, a strong faculty endorsement goes a long way to assuring administrative approval.

There are many ways to gain faculty support:

1.   A general mailing explaining the merits of a PIRG to all faculty members.

2.   Personal interviews with faculty members.

3.   Presentations to various faculty forums, such as the faculty senate, administrative councils, departmental meetings, etc.

It is important for supportive faculty members to let board members know what they think. They may want to write to the board as individuals or collectively as departments to register their support. A faculty petition may also be filed with the board when the students are presenting their case. If the board feels that the faculty will be involved with the PIRG, they may be more assured of its educational purposes.

In both Oregon and Minnesota, student organizers spent several months developing and adapting their plans before requesting administrative approval. Their final proposal included the following:

1.   A well-defined statement of purpose.

2.   An outline of the PIRG's organizational structure.

3.   An explanation of why a student-directed Public Interest Research Group is needed.

4.   A statement of the educational value of the PIRG.*

*Information on OSPIRG and MPIRG is available from these groups; see Appendix.

For many administrative boards, the educational value of the PIRG will be the decisive factor. Others will take the educational value for granted and focus on tax questions. (See Chapter 7 for an extended discussion of both these important questions.)

MODEL STATEMENT OF PURPOSE AND OBJECTIVES

___PIRG will undertake to identify and evaluate issues involving public policy decisions, including social planning, institutional regulation and control, and matters of individual rights which affect substantial numbers of people.   PIRG will determine the alternative solutions available, in order to determine what course of action ___PIRG should take to bring about corporate, governmental, and other institutional changes that are necessary to further the public interest.

Action taken by ___PIRG will consist of a coordinated effort of analysis and research; public education; active representation before legislative bodies and before administrative and regulatory agencies; and litigation—where such actions are warranted—to achieve the goals of this group. It will not become involved in internal campus disputes or disputes between campuses.

The general areas of ___PIRG concern will include consumer protection, resource planning, occupational safety, protection of natural areas and environmental quality, racial and sexual discrimination, landlord/ tenant relations, delivery of health care, freedom of information in government, and similar matters of urgent or long-range concern to the welfare of the people of the State of _____.

Besides educational or tax considerations, boards may inquire into aspects of the plan ranging from the propriety of using students fees to the validity of the signatures on the petitions. Some possible questions raised by board members may include the following:

1.   Will raising student fees for a Public Interest Research Group open the door for other student groups?

Because other groups may want to use the same petition process to raise fees to establish their own organizations, the board may fear that it will be deluged by similar requests. If other groups can gain overwhelming support from students, faculty, and many facets of the community, plus exhibit clearly the educational value in their programs, the board may well agree to raise student fees for those purposes, too. But the process itself eliminates all but the most determined groups. Therefore, it is doubtful that an unmanageable number of requests will come before the board. Those that do may be examined under the same standards applied to the PIRG.

2. Will the PIRG's refund provision force the university to offer refunds on other mandatory fees?

The answer is clearly no. Each fee request stands or falls on its own merits. There is no universal principle involved. A board can permit one fee to operate on the checkoff basis, another to be mandatory, and a third to offer refunds. Nevertheless, boards may worry about setting a precedent for refunding any fees at all.

This problem can be solved by placing the responsibility for refunding money with the PIRG and *not* with the university. The PIRG has a binding responsibility to offer a refund because this is the funding mechanism students approved. As far as the board is concerned, the fee increase is mandatory. However, if the PIRG offers the refund itself, the board does not set a binding precedent for refunding other mandatory fees.

3.   How does the board know that the petition signatures are valid?

Attesting to the validity of petition signatures can be done in several ways. In Oregon, students had a statistician take a random sample of two hundred signatures from each university and determine what percentage of that two hundred were registered students. This percentage was applied to the total number of petition signatures in order to determine the number of valid signatures. Another method of verification is to use a computer. Each signature is key-punched into a computer which cross-references each name with the list of duly enrolled students. The computer process is by far the most accurate, but the expense and time of punching out each name are significant. Organizers should weigh the benefits of each method carefully.

4.   How will the board know whether the students are supporting the PIRG a year from now?

Both OSPIRG and MPIRG provided in their articles of incorporation that any campus where 50 percent of the students requested refunds would no longer participate. This provision is an effective internal check on the PIRG as well as a good indicator of student response.

5.   How can students be involved in the plan besides paying the fee increase?

Obviously, not every student has the opportunity or the inclination to become involved actively in a PIRG project. There is no way that the professional staff, even with the help of interested faculty, can supervise the activities of more than a few hundred students at any one time. Therefore, the professional staff must seek out aggressive student leaders and train them to lead other students, if it is to achieve a multiplier effect and involve large masses of students.

Students who do work on projects may perform basic research and data-collection functions, or assist with legal brief-writing, or appear before state or municipal regulatory agencies. Additionally, the most interested students can run for election on local boards of directors or serve as volunteers working on local board committees. Students who are too busy to become actively involved, but who have areas of concern, can suggest projects to their local boards.

It is important that elections do not open splits among competing campus factions. At all times the focus of the PIRG must be offensive, directed away from campus issues toward public issues. A sure way to bring about an early collapse is to permit old rivalries to infiltrate and tear at the new group with intra-campus rivalries.

There are no certain formulas that guarantee administration approval. However, if the details of the plan have been thoroughly worked out and if strong student support has been received, most administrators find it difficult to deny students the right to work constructively to effect social betterment.

Election of the Local Board

Soon after approval is received, each participating

school should conduct an election to select representatives to the local board. Elections may be held independently or in conjunction with regular campus elections. School tradition usually determines election procedures.

Schools should schedule their elections on a rotating basis so that at no one time are more than half the schools holding elections. This insures that at least half the members of the state board are experienced. A complete turnover each election period would destroy the stability of the state board.

Recruiting and Hiring the Professional Staff

Thousands of presently employed professionals and graduating seniors are searching for work in the public interest arena. There are several ways to recruit these people to fill job openings in the PIRG. The best way to contact graduating seniors is a personal letter with an advertising flyer to university placement officers. Advertisements in *The New York Times, Los Angeles Times, The Washington Post,* and the leading state paper will reach already employed job seekers in major legal centers. MPIRG, for example, was overwhelmed with over three hundred résumés after a single advertisement in the Sunday *New York Times.*

Hiring should be done by members of the state board with faculty and community advisers providing support. The first position to fill is that of the staff director. Once the director is hired, he or she should participate in all other employment decisions.

Salary and contract terms vary depending on the experience of the individual and the wage scale of the area in which the group is located. Washington, D. C., PIRG attorneys earn forty-five hundred dollars per year, while MPIRG is paying its professionals ten thousand dollars per year, and OSPIRG is paying seventy-five hundred dollars.

The kinds of professional skills needed also vary. Since many of the remedies require action by courts or administrative agencies, lawyers should form the nucleus of the group. Especially in the early months of the PIRG, flexibility is essential. Each employee should be able to perform several different tasks.

7 TAX AND EDUCATION

Tax and educational considerations are paramount because they are the first and the highest hurdles the PIRGs have to clear to gain administrative approval. No board will sanction a student organization that might jeopardize the university's tax-exempt status. Similarly, most boards of education are empowered to authorize only educational activities. Therefore, unless the educational value of the PIRG can be demonstrated, the plan falls outside the purview of board authority and cannot be approved.

Tax Considerations *

A PIRG WILL BE A NONPROFIT, TAX-EXEMPT CORPORATION

A Public Interest Research Group must be organized and operated under the laws of the state in which it is located. The Secretary of State's office, usually located at

---

* The following explanation is not meant to be complete. A more comprehensive memorandum is available from the Washington, D. C., PIRG office. Because of the complexity of these questons, it is essential to enlist the aid of a law professor or community lawyer.

the state capitol, can supply information about the formation and operation of a nonprofit corporation. Since a nonprofit corporation which complies with appropriate Federal and state tax laws is eligible for "tax-exempt status," it will not be required to pay corporate income tax. Depending on its activities, a Public Interest Research Group can seek tax-exempt status under 26 United States Code 501 (c) 3 or under 26 United States Code 501 (c) 4:

> 501 (c) 3 status is granted to corporations organized and operated exclusively for "religious, charitable, scientific, testing for public safety, literacy or educational purposes. . ."

> 501 (c) 4 status is accorded to corporations "not organized for profit but operated exclusively for the promotion of social welfare."

SIMILARITIES AND DIFFERENCES BETWEEN 501 (c) 3 AND 501 (c) 4 STATUS

Besides granting tax exemption to corporations which qualify for either 501 (c) 3 or 501 (c) 4 status, the law gives an additional benefit to 501 (c) 3 corporations. Donors to these corporations are permitted to deduct the amount of their gift from their taxable income, thus lowering their personal income tax and giving them added incentive to make a contribution. No such privilege is accorded 501 (c) 4 corporations. Because of the tax benefits it conveys to both the corporation and its patrons, 501 (c) 3 status is harder to acquire.

IS 501 (c) 3 OR 501 (c) 4 STATUS PREFERABLE FOR
A STUDENT PIRG?

The answer to this question depends on how the PIRG
intends to function. A PIRG with 501 (c) 4 status can
lobby freely, litigate in almost every area, and conduct
citizen organizing drives, but it cannot receive foundation funding or provide tax benefits to wealthy community residents who may donate money.

A PIRG with a 501 (c) 3 status can carry on public
education efforts, litigate in many areas, research any
issue, and confer a tax benefit for all donations, but
cannot devote any substantial part of its activities to
lobbying or to organizing efforts which would result in
lobbying.

Obviously, 501 (c) 3 status would not benefit a student-supported PIRG because the three or four dollars
each student donates is too small to amount to a significant tax savings. Since student contributions normally
provide adequate support, the other 501 (c) 3 asset—
foundation support—is canceled out by the loss of such
important areas of action as lobbying and organizing
citizens to lobby.

Based on these considerations, 501 (c) 4 status is
probably the best form of organization for a student-
supported Public Interest Research Group.

The benefit of tax deductability is significant only when
donations are large. Foundations normally do not make
grants to corporations which do not have 501 (c) 3

status, and wealthy donors usually want the benefit of personal tax deduction when they make gifts, which only a 501 (c) 3 corporation gives them.

At the same time that the law grants benefits, it also imposes certain constraints. Neither 501 (c) 3 nor 501 (c) 4 corporations may intervene in any political campaign on behalf of a candidate for public office. A 501 (c) 4 corporation may lobby freely and support or oppose legislation, but 501 (c) 3 status severely restricts lobbying. A *public* 501 (c) 3 organization can devote only an "insubstantial" part of its activities to lobbying. A *private* 501 (c) 3 group cannot lobby at all. ("Public" 501 (c) 3 status is accorded a 501 (c) 3 group that receives more than one-third of its contributions from the general public. "Private" status is granted to corporations supported by a few major contributors.)

The amount of money spent on lobbying is not a sufficient criterion to determine its substantiality; instead, all resources and activities of the corporation must be examined in relation to IRS standards.

An additional possibility under consideration by students in Oregon and Minnesota involves setting up two separate corporations. One corporation would apply for 501 (c) 3 status and carry out research, public education, and litigation (as permitted by the applicable tax law), while the other would seek 501 (c) 4 status for lobbying and other types of litigation. The 501 (c) 3 corporation would be able to attract foundation support, while the 501 (c) 4 corporation could carry out lobby-

ing efforts and other litigation. Although this arrangement is feasible, it is not wise. A student PIRG simply
does not need such support. Foundation money should
be left for public interest groups which cannot get money
any other way.

LEGAL STATUS OF UNIVERSITIES IN RELATION TO PIRG

All universities and colleges are tax-exempt corporations supported in part by private donations from individuals and foundations. The tax-deductibility of their
gifts is essential. Private schools are also tax-exempt
501 (c) 3 corporations, and state schools, while they may
have 501 (c) 3 status, are normally tax-exempt because
they are institutions of the state. So a major question
in the minds of most college administrators, regents,
and trustees is whether the tax-exempt status of the
institution could be jeopardized by any activities of
the PIRG. The answer for both private and state schools
is a resounding no.

If the PIRG is a 501 (c) 3 corporation, the question
should never arise, since the activities of a 501 (c) 3
corporation do not adversely affect the tax status of another 501 (c) 3 corporation or of a state instrumentality.
If the PIRG should exceed the permissible bounds of activity for a 501 (c) 3 corporation and engage in "substantial" lobbying activities or incorporate with a 501 (c)
4 status, the question still does not apply to schools
which are considered state institutions. Such institutions

have no restrictions on their lobbying activities. Private schools, however, cannot afford to risk their 501 (c) 3 status.

Private universities will endanger their status *only* if they engage in a "substantial" amount of lobbying activities. Certainly 15 percent of an institution's activities would be viewed as substantial, but 1 percent probably would not. In general, a 5-percent rule is applied as a rough test and, as the next paragraphs will show, it would be difficult if not impossible for a PIRG to make up more than 1 percent of university activity.

Two points must be made with respect to the activities of a PIRG. First, the university only acts as a collecting agent for the research group. The money collected belongs to the PIRG; the university, while it has possession, has no control over the money. The money itself, and the activities it supports, are those of PIRG, not the university. Therefore, the status of the PIRG should in no way affect the university's own tax status if the university is only a collecting agent for the PIRG.

Second, even if the money were considered to belong to the university and the PIRG devoted all of its resources to lobbying, its activities would still not constitute a "substantial" portion of the university's total activities. A contribution of three to four dollars per student per year adds up to less than one-tenth of 1 percent of the school's total revenues. When all the resources and activities of the university are considered, this figure is even smaller. Therefore, neither a 501 (c) 3 nor a 501

(c) 4 PIRG endangers a private university's tax-exempt status.

The Educational Value of a PIRG
RESEARCH

The PIRG's major projects are under the direction of the professional staff, in consultation with faculty and community resource persons. However, much of the actual study is done by students, either during the academic year or during vacation periods.

The main thrust of the PIRG's research is obtaining existing information in the area under investigation. This research includes gathering documents, searching through government files, interviewing public officials, conducting statistical surveys, collecting samples, and performing laboratory analysis. Its educational value is obvious.

Too often in colleges and in universities theoretical constructs are erected with no grounding in empirical research. In a real sense, the PIRG serves as a bridge between theory and practice. For example, students researching a utility rate regulating agency or examining the biological effect of a particular pollutant in an estuary environment are forced to perform the most exacting kind of research before arriving at a conclusion that can be presented publicly to the press, legislature, or an administrative agency. Even learning *how* to do such research is a major educational benefit.

Further, the PIRG concept is built on the idea of interdisciplinary study. When any problem is researched, every possible angle must be examined and all interrelationships discovered. A single lawyer or a single group of biology students cannot hope to be able to research all sides of a problem. Hence, students from a broad spectrum of backgrounds, as well as a diverse group of professionals, are a requisite for the PIRG's success. Many science-oriented students tend to ignore liberal arts studies because of their "lack of relevance." Concurrently, many liberal arts majors feel that science is a complicated morass of cells, instruments, and technical jargon without human values. Consequently, the communication patterns between students in divergent disciplines are frequently superficial at best, if not nonexistent. The PIRG involvement provides a new impetus for interdisciplinary study.

In the same vein, the PIRG offers students from different institutions an opportunity to work together on common problems. Also, students are able to draw on the expertise of faculty on other campuses where a particular discipline or research program is emphasized. This consideration has unlimited potential to open channels of communication between students and faculty, between academic institutions, and between educational disciplines.

PUBLIC EDUCATION

An important educational consideration is the involvement of members of the community with the functions of the PIRG. Too often in the past, the citizenry has remained isolated from the universities and, as a result, has received a false or misleading impression of higher education. And too often students have been isolated from the activities and concerns of the ordinary citizen. Working together on projects of common concern facilitates a better understanding and develops rapport between students and the general public.

Students also gain valuable experience in the use of the public media to educate other students, the university, and the general public. This is accomplished through the use of public forums, local television and radio programs, and by publicizing projects in campus, local, and state newspapers.

ADVOCACY

The key to a PIRG is effective advocacy for the public interest in policy decisions made by executive, legislative, and judicial bodies. The advocacy function of the PIRG is carried out primarily by the professional staff in two basic areas: administrative and legislative bodies, and courts of law.

Some students, especially those in graduate and professional schools, are particularly suited to aid the staff in its advocacy functions. Students involved at this level of the PIRG activity are called upon to testify before legislative and administrative hearings, draft model legislation and prepare legal memoranda, and do legal research. These action programs provide students with a valuable operational knowledge of the existing channels for social change as well as empirical experience.

8 SOME PUBLIC INTEREST PROBLEMS AND SOLUTIONS

When student energy is coupled with professional skills, major changes can be accomplished. There are numerous areas where their efforts may make important differences in the formation of laws, the implementation of laws, the behavior of corporations, the responsiveness of government, and the lives of people. The following projects are offered as suggestions for a student PIRG's action program. Naturally, there are many other projects that will arise from the special circumstances in a state or region.

Some of these projects may also be undertaken by individuals or groups without a PIRG. Not all students are organizers nor are students in every state ready to form a PIRG. Much can be done even where the broad base of a student organization does not exist. Indeed, there are projects that should not be undertaken by a PIRG. Foremost among those is investigation of the universities themselves. A PIRG should direct its energies outward from the campuses to society at large, not only to avoid an "ivory-tower" syndrome, and not only because, in any impartial evaluation of American society, it should be clear that the greater and more pressing problems are off-campus, but also because directing the energies and resources of a PIRG inward to the university is almost sure to destroy the PIRG: (1) few universities will be willing to permit a fee increase to support an organization that may turn against them, and (2) investigation of the university itself will, as experience in non-PIRG cases has often shown, split the student body, destroying the unity of purpose that is essential if the PIRG is to support itself. The PIRG should direct itself to the broad public interest; other groups may focus inward.

In most cases, attempts to do so by reforming an agency or implementing a piece of legislation require long-term efforts that individuals or *ad hoc* groups cannot provide. These attempts may also require litigation or a process of administration action that also requires resources most individuals lack. In these cases, it is essential that a PIRG be available to go the last step that is often most crucial in really affecting the problem.

Property Tax Project

About 85 percent of locally raised revenues, and about 48 percent of combined state and local revenues, come from property taxes. This means that the quality of schools, sanitation, police, health and environmental protection, and other services which a local government can provide depends in large measure upon this one tax.

Property taxes are also important to the "private" business sector. The profitability of a commercial building, a speculative investment in vacant land, and even a large industrial property can be heavily influenced by the level of the property taxes upon it.

The combination of these two forces—the need of the community for tax revenues, and the desire of businessmen for maximal profit—can bring an intense pressure to bear upon the administration of the tax. And frequently the administration is not strong enough to withstand it. One leading scholar has written ". . . the general property tax as actually administered is beyond all doubt one of the worst taxes known in the civilized world." The tax is commonly administered by elected assessors, untrained and underpaid, who frequently have business and political ties to real estate and business interests in the community. As a result, the social, economic, and political powers in a community quite often leave their footprints upon the administration of the local property tax. The study of the tax is really a window through which to see the use and abuse of other forms of power in local government.

Some particular access points which citizen groups might explore are the following:

CONFLICTS OF INTEREST

Assessment offices and local property tax appeals boards are frequently laden with realtors, real estate developers, apartment building owners, construction company executives, and insurance men. (Zoning boards, it should be noted, are also so constituted.) These men are in a position to use their public office to advance their private business interests. Citizens could study how these men have acted or voted upon properties in which they might have a business interest.

Some states, it should be noted, have conflict-of-interest laws and codes of ethics which prohibit officials from acting in matters in which they have a private financial interest. The New York Attorney General has ruled that under New York law a realtor is barred from acting as local assessor.

INCOMPETENCE AND MALADMINISTRATION

Some assessors have no background or training. They spend little time on their job, rarely reassess properties, and raise assessments only when properties are bought and sold, or new buildings are constructed. Assessment records may be kept in an informal manner, and in pencil, so that they can be "adjusted" or changed at whim.

Citizens have a vital stake in the efficiency and competence of property tax administration. It is highly relevant to know how qualified the local assessor is, how he goes about his work, and whether his operating procedures and record-keeping measure up to legal requirements.

EXEMPTIONS

A property tax exemption is a form of hidden subsidy.

Prepare a list of all the exempt properties in your community and ask, "Should the people of this community be supporting these property owners?"

Abuse of exemptions fall into two categories. First, exemptions are often granted to those not legally entitled to them. Common examples are income-producing properties of supposedly nonprofit organizations such as churches, clubs, and educational institutions. Check to see if the office building owned by a fraternal organization and rented out to private businesses is exempt from property taxes as a "meeting hall." Or see if the vacant land that churches and schools have been holding for years while it grows in value is off the tax rolls as land used for "educational or religious purposes."

Some exemptions are within the letter of the property tax law but are questionable on other grounds. Is a country club which practices racial or religious discrimination eligible for a state subsidy in the form of an exemption from property taxes?

Granting property tax exemptions to groups that do not really need them constitutes another abuse. In such cases the rich simply get a free ride. In some states "veterans" and "homestead" exemptions erase a good measure of the property tax liability of wealthy home owners. Real estate developers and speculators in land often use so-called "farm land" assessment laws to minimize their tax bills while their land "ripens" for development. Private businesses often ride home free on exempt state- or Federally-owned property by leasing it from the government.

PUBLIC ACCESS TO PROPERTY TAX
INFORMATION

Property tax records should be public records, so that citizens can check on the integrity of the assessing and taxing function, and so that taxpayers can determine if they have been treated unfairly and then compile the evidence with which to win a case in court. There are state laws requiring that certain records be kept open to the public.

But frequently local assessors establish little tyrannies over their domains. They create complex procedures which effectively frustrate citizen efforts to see records. They keep the records in a form which no one but they themselves can understand.

It is important, then, to find out what records are and are not available. Ask to see the assessment rolls, the assessor's "work sheets," his tax maps, and the manuals provided by the state detailing the rules he is supposed to follow in establishing values for property. The work sheets are especially important. They show *how* the assessor actually arrived at a given value. Without them, taxpayers have no way of proving that the assessor did not observe the procedures he is legally bound to follow.

Also important are records of reductions and appeals. Is there a record of all such appeals? Is the amount of the reduction given, along with an explanation? If no such records are kept, the assessor and/or the Board of Appeals can dole out assessment reductions at will, without being accountable to legal standards or public scrutiny.

UNDERASSESSMENT

Corruption of the property tax system most frequently appears in the form of underassessment. Sometimes only individual properties are underassessed—the home of a political crony, the business property of a friend or business partner. But at other times whole classes of property are underassessed. Neighborhoods of white home owners may be underassessed in comparison to neighborhoods where blacks reside, largely because political power resides in the white neighborhood. Large industrial and commercial properties may win underassessments through their economic power or political influence.

Most state constitutions require, in effect, that property be assessed at "full market value" or some variant of that phrase. But courts have held that assessments do not have to be at *full* market value as long as all taxpayers pay an equal percentage of full market value. Thus to prove underassessment, one must show that some property owners are paying a lower percentage of full market value than others are.

Assessed values are fairly easy to determine from the local assessment records. But determining full fair market value may pose problems. Residential property is the easiest to work with. Sales figures are the most reliable standard of full market value, and residential property is bought and sold frequently. With a little ingenuity, students should be able to approximate a rough full market value for almost any residential property, and then compare the ratio of the assessed property to the full value on that property (the "assessment ratio") to the ratios for other residential properties in the jurisdiction.

Commercial and industrial properties are harder to work with. They are bought and sold less frequently; and especially in the case of industrial properties, they tend to be unique. Nevertheless, there are ways to approximate full market values. Local realtors and appraisers may be helpful in arriving at estimates. For industrial property, check annual reports, company publicity, and labor union publications to find out how much capital investment has gone into particular plants over particular years. Then see how much the assessment has gone up in those years. In addition, insurance companies often have rules of thumb for estimating the amount of capital investment necessary to produce a given output of goods.

Another approach is to ignore the assessments on buildings and improvements, and work with land values only. Get a tax map from the assessor's office or from a private mapping firm. If the assessment records are broken down between land and buildings, determine the land assessment per square foot of each lot. When the mapping of a particular area is completed, the cases of underassessment should be apparent.

In looking for the underassessments in a community,

the patterns to be alert for are favors to political supporters, to particular businesses or to large businesses
generally, to politically powerful residential neighborhoods, and to properties in which assessment or local
government officials have an economic interest. Vacant
land is also often underassessed. Sometimes when improvements are made on vacant land, they do not even
appear on the assessor's records.

TAXPAYERS' ORGANIZATIONS

In more than one community, the so-called "taxpayers' organization" has been taken over by the entrenched
political and economic powers of the community. Such
leadership focuses the group's attention on cutting down
local government expenditures—usually for schools—and
diverts it entirely from studies of whether everyone in the
community is bearing his fair share of the tax load.

It would be a service to the community to lay bare the
real nature of the group that is supposed to be serving
it. Who are the leaders? What are their business and political connections? Does the leadership observe the
group's own bylaws? What issues has the group pro-
moted? What issues has it shied away from?

RESOURCE PEOPLE

Resource people have to be chosen from those outside
the local "establishment." One or two knowledgeable
mavericks can be a tremendous asset. Sometimes even

a person within the "establishment" can cooperate secretly. People to look for are lawyers, local government officials, *retired* government officials, candidates defeated in recent elections, realtors, appraisers, newspaper reporters, and the like.

RESOURCE TOOLS

Resource tools include the following: land-use and tax maps, available from the assessor's office or from private mapping and appraisal firms; assessment roles and the assessor's work sheets; deeds; state handbooks for use by assessors; real estate pages of local newspapers; aerial photographs.

Perhaps the two most potent resource tools are lawsuits and publicity. Even the threats of these can do wonders.

Occupational Safety and Health Project

Student PIRGs can help workers enforce their rights to a safe and healthful work environment. Each year at least 15,000 workers are killed from work-related injuries; two and one-half million more are disabled and a total of eight million injured. A recent Department of Labor-sponsored survey indicates that there probably are 25 million injuries each year. No one knows how many diseases really occur but surveys indicate that millions are exposed to excess levels of contaminants which result in shortening of life expectancy and possible long-term harmful effects such as genetic damage or the onslaught of diseases after retirement. The problem of occupational disease is equally serious to that of job injuries. Many workers suffer from the gases, dusts, fumes, and other contaminants they encounter in their work environment. The Department of Health, Education and Welfare estimates at least 390,000 cases of occupational disease each year, but this is acknowledged as only the tip of the problem because many diseases are not officially identified or not reported. Many job injuries are not reported either.

One reason that occupational health and safety is a mounting problem is the rapidity with which new chemicals are introduced into the industrial process. What effects many of these substances have on workers are still unknown. Generally they are presumed safe until proven otherwise. Even in areas where the hazards are known, the problems remain because workers' rights to health and safety have largely gone unrecognized or unenforced.

The Occupational Safety and Health Act passed December 29, 1970 gives workers a means of protection through government standards and enforcement. The Act protects nearly all workers since it covers all businesses having an effect on commerce, except where another Federal agency or the Department of Labor has been given statutory authority to carry out its own occupational safety and health programs. At present, this law applies to an estimated 57 million workers and 4.1 million work places.

The Act directs the Secretary of Labor to establish

standards for occupational health and safety within two years after passage of the law. Interim but generally inadequate standards are in effect now. The Secretary is also directed to approve plans submitted by states that wish to assume responsibility for development and/or enforcement of standards if they meet the requirements of the Act. At the present time, the Department of Labor's actions in implementing the new law show that the Department is attempting to relinquish its enforcement responsibility to the states without requiring that the states first develop adequate state plans. However, since the Federal law requires each state plan to be "at least as effective" as the Federal plan, student PIRGs can be very valuable in documenting whether or not state procedures actually comply with Section 18 (c) of the Federal Acts. The first step in effective student monitoring of the compliance of either state or Federal governments is to acquire a copy of the Federal Act. Any deviation from its terms by the Department of Labor or the state should be reported immediately to affected labor unions, if any, and to the Chairmen of the House and Senate Committees on Labor.

The law provides that each covered employer has a general duty to furnish employment free from "recognized hazards" causing or likely to cause death or serious harm to workers, even if such hazards are not covered by a standard. "Serious harm" is broadly defined by the Federal law, so as to include any expected diminution of a worker's life or work life.

The Act will not be effective, however, without significant pressure from workers and other citizens for meaningful enforcement. Fortunately, there are a number of ways the public and the affected worker can take part in enforcement of the law. Here is where student PIRGs can be effective.

1. A major problem confronting workers is their inability to identify health and safety hazards. Student PIRGs can set up programs for analyzing dusts from the work environment of a particular plant or industry to identify substances that may be harmful to workers' health. The workers or the union, if any, can authorize the students to collect samples, or can give them product samples for analysis. Research may be done both by professionals on the full-time staff and by students, who may make the research part of a laboratory project.

When hazardous substances are discovered, the results can be used to demonstrate the need for a new standard or amendment of an existing one, through procedures established under the Act. Or an analysis may determine that dust levels in a particular plant exceed the standard and the employer is in violation of the law. Here the Act provides ways for instigating enforcement procedures.

2. A student PIRG can also operate a voluntary service for workers. Part of the service may be devoted to education. For example, the PIRG could teach workers how to use audiometers to measure the noise levels in their work places and document cases where the law is being violated. Since it is often difficult for outsiders to gain access to plants, much of the initial data collection

and detection of hazards will be left to workers them-selves; however, students can assist workers in develop-ing the best methods to collect data or detect problems. Many students can be found on campus who have worked in unhealthful or hazardous jobs during sum-mers and can lend their knowledge and assistance.

3.   A PIRG-organized voluntary service can also test workers for symptoms of occupational disease. Some-times this will save a worker's health. For example, if textile workers receive regular medical tests they can be warned when they have the early states of "brown lung," a chronic lung disease caused by breathing cotton dust, and the disease can be arrested. In addition, the tests can demonstrate the need for greater protection for workers. Regular medical examinations should be pro-vided by employers, but many fail to do so. Public health or medical students working with individual work-ers or union locals can set up a testing program.. HEW can be contacted for information on safety and health criteria and can also be requested to make investigation and to require the employer to monitor the levels of dan-gerous substances in the air of the work place.

4.   When standards are proposed they will be based on criteria developed by HEW. These criteria are the HEW recommendations as to standards necessary to assure that no employee will suffer "impaired health, diminished life expectancy or diminished functional capacity" even if he is exposed to the levels recommended for his entire adult working life. Student PIRGs should

be prepared to challenge the HEW criteria by submitting evidence and recommendations to HEW before the criteria are finalized, and to initiate HEW action to set criteria. Then, when the Department of Labor appoints advisory committees to set standards, student PIRGs should monitor this process and recommend qualified faculty or community health experts to assure no unjustified weakening of standards. A student PIRG can monitor this process by submitting comments and data to the Secretary of Labor.

Student PIRGs should examine the 1970 Occupational Safety and Health Act, and their own resources, in setting up a program. They may want to challenge a state program where the state is trying to take over enforcement of the Act with an inadequate plan.

The U.S. Department of Labor, Washington, D.C., can provide information on the Act. For information on research into occupational disease, write to the Bureau of Occupational Health, U.S. Department of Health, Education, and Welfare, Washington, D.C. The state AFL-CIO will also have materials and information on enforcing the rights of workers under the Act.

Employment Discrimination

Title VII of the Civil Rights Act of 1964 forbids employment discrimination on grounds of race, sex, creed, or national origin. Executive Order 11246 as amended by 11375 goes a step further and requires all companies doing business with the government to take "affirmative action" to hire women and members of minorities. However, it is safe to say that virtually every major United States corporation violates these laws in one or more ways.

To comply with these Executive Orders, a company doing business with the government must do more than hire a respectable quota of black janitors and women secretaries. Such an employer must seek out minority groups and women to fill jobs at all levels in the company, including management. The scarcity of women and minorities in middle and upper management positions is testimony to corporate disregard for these laws.

Students can help insure compliance with civil rights laws in several ways. A single complaint to the Equal Employment Opportunities Commission (EEOC) may generate a major EEOC investigation which will uncover additional instances of employment discrimination.

Many cities and states have Human Rights Commissions that handle similar charges. Students can investigate the employment practices of local banks, construction companies, or department stores. The phone company is often a good place to start. Based on the number of complaints received by the EEOC and the evidence of government investigations, the Bell system is the largest sex discriminator in the country. When discrimination is found, charges can be brought before the local agency or, if satisfaction is not received, the EEOC can be asked to intervene.

Investigations frequently require ingenuity. For example, a group of New York University law students were assured by state officials and construction contractors that blacks accounted for 20 percent of the labor force on construction projects in New York State. The students went to construction sites where they counted the number and noted the color of all workers entering the sites. Their figure of blacks on the labor force turned out to be less than 5 percent. The students' effort resulted in extensive newspaper coverage, temporarily halted construction on one major building site, and forced acceleration in minority hiring programs.

For more information on employment discrimination and citizen remedies, write to the local state employment office or the EEOC, 1800 G Street, N.W., Washington, D.C. 20006.

Environmental Projects

Universities in every part of the country, whether urban or rural, are surrounded by symptoms of a deteriorating environment. Near one campus, a factory belches acrid smoke. Another is neighbor to a ticky-tacky urban sprawl, and a third borders an open sewer that once was a trout stream. Air, water, and noise pollution are national problems, and students everywhere can establish effective environmental action programs to combat them. In the past, many environmental groups have been all too willing to take stands on large national issues but reluctant to undertake positive action on serious local problems.

The range of possible action programs is limitless. The following is a capsule list of some possible projects:

WATER POLLUTION

Dumping industrial wastes in a river without a permit from the Army Corps of Engineers violates the 1899 Water Refuse Act. This Act requires United States Attorneys to bring suit if unpermitted wastes are being dumped into navigable waters. If the U.S. Attorney does not act, a private citizen is permitted to bring the suit and, when successful, collect half of the total amount the company is fined.

Congressman Henry Reuss, House Office Building, Washington, D.C., will send on request a free kit detailing how to bring such a suit. Following his simple instructions, student environmental groups can put a stop to unsanctioned water pollution.

LEAD PAINT POISONING

Chips of lead-base paint are a serious health hazard. Eaten usually by small children, they can lead to brain damage, mental retardation, and, in some cases, death. The problem of lead poisoning from paint is most acute in low-income-area homes. Here, landlords in many cases continue to use paint with large amounts of lead because it is the cheapest paint they can buy. When they switch to better-quality paints for repainting, the problem of lead poisoning remains. Under the new layers of low-lead paint are the many layers of high-lead paint from previous years. When the paint chips and peels, not only the new paint comes off but much of the old. Repainting is not enough.

Students can detect lead in paint chips rapidly and accurately by using equipment available in the chemistry departments of most universities. Where dangerous levels of lead are found, the landlords and tenants should be alerted of the hazard.

Analyses can also detect actual lead poisoning. Detection at an early stage can prevent serious brain damage. Urine, blood, or hair samples are needed for analysis, and students working with public health teams or community clinics can help gather and analyze these samples.

If they find a high correlation between the use of lead-based paints and actual cases of lead poisoning, students can prepare actions against the landlords who permit unhealthy and potentially fatal conditions to exist. They can alert the Housing Authority, prepare legislation, or bring a suit against the worst offenders.

AIR POLLUTION

In December of 1970, Congress passed the Clean Air Act (Public Law 91-604), the strongest air pollution legislation in its history. In order for this Act to be effective, enforcement must be strong and uncompromising.

The Clean Air Act of 1970 contains four important provisions for controlling air pollution from stationary sources.

1. It authorizes the administrator of the Environ-

mental Protection Agency to establish national emission standards for many basic pollutants.

2. After these standards have been set, no person may construct any new pollution source which will exceed the air quality standards.

3. The administrator of the Environmental Protection Agency may grant a waiver giving a polluter up to two years to comply with the·standards if he finds this period necessary for the installation of controls and believes that steps will be taken to protect the health of persons from "imminent endangerment."

4. The Environmental Protection Agency must scrutinize each state's procedure for implementing and enforcing the emission standards for hazardous air pollutants.

Environmental groups can be invaluable in insuring that these provisions are administered in the public interest. These groups can be especially valuable in watchdogging a state's enforcement plan. If procedures developed by a state are unnecessarily complicated, or if other provisions of the Clean Air Act are ignored, a formal complaint may be filed with the Environmental Protection Agency. The complaint may result in a revision of state standards or a compliance order from the Environmental Protection Agency.

The same watchdog function is necessary to insure that waivers to the pollution standards are only granted to industries which qualify under the Act.

In all, the Clean Air Act can be a powerful tool for

cleaning up our fouled air. However, any legislation is only as strong as its enforcement. By monitoring the state and Federal agencies responsible for enforcement, environmental groups can take a large step toward cleaner air.

Consumer Action Centers

Most consumers, on some occasion, buy short-weighted meat, defective appliances, poorly contructed furniture, or bad service. They may be victims of fraudulent credit schemes, deceptive advertisements, or cleverly worded warranties. For some, the fraud is perennial and especially serious. The poor, the under-educated, the ignorant, those with language difficulties, migrant workers, the very young, and the very old are most often hardest hit.

To complicate matters, consumer fraud constitutes an unusually complex area of the law. Prosecution is rare and difficult at best. The result creates a morass where the consumer finds it easier to give up than to pursue his rights. Although there may be a number of local agencies already at work for the consumer, few are completely effective, and the problems have grown so massive that a student consumer group has ample opportunity to make a meaningful contribution.

A student consumer action center can handle all types of complaints, or it can specialize in particular areas such as automobile safety or supermarkets. The cost of a center is minimal; the only expense need be for phone and stationery. Newspapers and radio and television stations ordinarily provide free public service time to advertise the center's programs, and they are often eager to pass along consumer information.

Consumer centers can perform some or all of the following services:

1. Conduct consumer education programs explaining credit costs, unit pricing, comparison shopping, and the like.

2. Research advertising claims, food quality, credit policies, or pricing patterns in rich and poor areas of the city.

3. Investigate warranty claims to see whether they are honored by local automobile dealers.

4. Train consumer advocates to represent consumers in disputes with manufacturers or retailers.

5. Set up a consumer complaint phone number to give individual consumers a means of voicing complaints. All complaints would then be referred to the appropriate governmental agency or investigated by the staff of the center.

6. Organize picketing or other forms of legal last recourse protest against unscrupulous merchants.

7. Develop consumer programs for local radio and television stations.

8. Start a consumer library.

To set up a center, students should seek advice from

faculty members or from local consumer protection groups. For more information, write to:

> Consumer Action Centers
> P. O. Box 28108
> Central Station
> Washington, D. C. 20005

Retail Price Comparisons

Most consumers are unable to conduct market surveys to determine comparative prices. Consequently, buying decisions are made with inadequate information or solely on the basis of geographical proximity to a particular store. The store owner, however, is well aware of competitors' prices. Major grocery chains receive competitors' prices through state and Federal government market surveys. Other retail establishments receive the same information or have the resources to compile their own surveys. Trade associations help members to exchange price information. Meanwhile, the consumer, unorganized and without extensive resources, is caught in an information gap.

To make rational purchasing decisions consumers need the same information as retailers. Comparative price surveys are one method that will enable the public to pierce through the gimmickry of deceptive marketing techniques to make an impact on the price structure. As it stands, consumers are supposed to compare prices on their own without the benefit of computerized government market surveys. If consumers collected and shared information in some organized fashion, the individual buyer would be placed on a more equal footing with retailers.

A student PIRG has the resources to organize regular consumer price surveys on local or statewide bases. The system would operate in the following way:

1. Students would draw up a representative list of items and survey the prices of those items at major retail outlets and selected neighborhood stores.
2. The lists would be fed into a computer for fast data analysis.
3. The computer output would be a comparison of prices which would reveal not only specific item price differences, but the overall pricing policies of the chain of stores.

The Hawaii state government has funded such a project since April 1969. On Wednesday of each week, the day specials go into effect, paid surveyors of the Hawaii Food Price Study survey eighty-five items in each of twenty-five stores. Results of the survey are printed in Honolulu's Friday morning newspaper, listing store totals for an abbreviated list of forty items. The results also showed which store had the lowest price for each individual item. The survey rekindled vigorous competition in the area, to the point where stores specifically lowered prices on the surveyed items to better their ranking in the survey. To counter these tactics the survey added fifteen items to the list (which then contained seventy items) that changed from week to week, so no store would know exactly which items would be surveyed. The results of this work demonstrated that three new discount chains had prices averaging 9 percent below the established chains, and showed a total price spread of 18 percent from the lowest to highest stores surveyed. Because these facts were published weekly, the major food chains were forced to lower their prices, bringing down the average food cost in Hawaii by 4 percent. During the same period, mainland food prices rose by 2 percent.

Washington, D.C., consumer groups are utilizing a similar system to gather grocery prices. Each Washington surveyor spends about forty-five minutes gathering price information in a single store and phoning in results. The computer tabulates the results in a matter of minutes. In addition to recording price differences on selected items, the Washington survey is programmed to check price differences between inner city and suburban stores, to search for fraudulent practices in advertised specials, and to isolate which store offers the best bargains. By gathering this information on a regular basis, Washington consumer groups hope to hold down prices and to spot effective inflation, which occurs when item size is reduced without a corresponding reduction in price.

The grocery industry lends itself well to price comparisons because prices change week to week. But the methodology of the survey can be used equally well in price surveys of drug stores, appliance dealers, and other retail establishments on a weekly or monthly basis. In addition, surveys of items that are of seasonal interest could be compared when they are most in demand. For example, toys could be priced during the Christmas season.

Price comparisons are only useful if they are widely disseminated. Newspapers, radio and television consumer reports, and consumer newsletters can help to spread the word. Mimeographed handouts may be distributed as well. It is possible that the commercial media will pay for this service which can offset the cost of computer time.

A package has been developed to help groups organize price comparisons in their own area. Included in this package is a manual explaining the methods for getting a survey started and the computer program used by the Washington, D.C., survey.

For further information and a copy of these materials contact:

Mark Fredricksen
P. O. Box 19567
Washington, D.C. 20036

9 SOME FINAL THOUGHTS

Successful student-supported research groups should breed similar organizations in the general community. Chapters of the League of Woman Voters, for example, could supplement their own efforts by hiring full-time advocates for the public interest. Women and blacks could organize a PIRG to guarantee their right to equality. Urban residents intent on protecting their right to breathe could form a PIRG to fight air pollution.

The foundations for such efforts already exist. For instance, automobile owners could turn their moribund automobile clubs into advocates for health and safety. Each AAA chapter could hire its own staff of lawyers to protect the consumer and environmental rights of its members.

Unions could devote some fraction of the interest earned by their pension funds to hire doctors who would work for occupational health safeguards. They could also develop group legal services for their members as some unions are contemplating doing.

Lawyers could organize public interest law firms. In New York, Los Angeles, Washington, D. C., and Chicago, young lawyers have taken a first step in this direction. Law councils in each of these cities have been organized to examine public problems. The next step is for the councils to hire their own staff attorneys.

In some areas, the public interest movement has already started. Sport and commercial fishermen, through the Fishermen's Clean Water Action Project, are raising money to support a professional team to combat water pollution. Airline travelers have banded together under the Aviation Consumer Action Program, which seeks to penetrate the maze of airline regulations to secure rights for the passenger and protect his welfare.

Some states have also begun to form citizen-based groups. In the spring of 1970, high school and college students in Connecticut, organized by attorneys from the Washington, D.C., PIRG staff and aided by community groups and individual citizens, raised almost fifty thousand dollars from contributions to form the Connecticut Citizen Action Group. Citizen Action has hired a five-member staff, including three attorneys, to press for environmental quality and other public interest issues.

The Ohio Public Interest Action Group (OPIAG), which was formed at the same time, is using the eighty-five thousand dollars it raised to hire a staff of eight public interest activists. During their first year CCAG and OPIAG will be directed by Ralph Nader and

members of the Washington, D. C., PIRG. Thereafter
they will operate independently. Individual cities and
towns in both Ohio and Connecticut are considering
hiring environmental ombudsmen to protect their air
and water.

Even with the formation of these groups, however,
the public interest movement needs accelerating, and
there is plenty of room to expand the student PIRG
concept. Presently, student-supported Public Interest
Research Groups are operating exclusively on the
state level. Yet state legislatures and regulatory agencies
are not always the proper forums for action. Frequently,
jurisdiction lies with the Federal government. In these
cases it would be advantageous to have a full-time
lobbyist or public interest lawyer in Washington, D. C.
Such a full-time representative could monitor the activities of the state delegation as well as press for
public interest issues in Federal agencies.

Another way to expand the student PIRG concept
would be to create a single Washington organization
serving the needs of several state-based PIRGs. Each
PIRG could contribute to the salary and overhead
expenses of one full-time public interest professional.
The staff would work on problems common to all
states, such as tax reform, Federal health and education legislation, social security and welfare measures,
and Federal environmental and consumer legislation.

There are endless permutations of these plans, but
they all rest on the basic recognition that unless citizens

become active in the areas where decisions are rendered, those decisions will not be responsive to citizen needs. Rather, they will continue to be made in isolation behind the closed doors of administrative agencies, in executive sessions of public bodies with little or no citizen input, or in corporate board rooms. Until this kind of secrecy can be removed, the person who reads *The New York Times,* votes regularly, and writes an occasional letter to his legislator will never be a match for a full-time lobbyist. Secrecy and hidden processes cater to special interest representatives who have both the expertise and the economic incentive to force access into decision-making arenas. The unheroic, ordinary citizen is closed out, but the formation of student-supported Public Interest Research Groups provides representation for him.

Additionally, PIRGs make possible the emergence of a new class of public citizen—men and women whose full-time employment is in the public interest arena. Each year, college and professional school graduates search vainly for public interest jobs. Unfortunately, few exist. As a result, there is a steady procession of unenthusiastic workers, marching from classroom to corporation. PIRGs provide alternative careers for citizen advocates serving the public interest.

The work of the PIRG may change as the mood of the campus shifts and as rotating student directors inject new issues of concern. This movement insures growth, vitality, and relevance. But, though the issues may change, there remains always the continuing need for effective citizen participation to insure that the governmental and corporate processes are responsive to the public interest.

APPENDIX

OREGON STUDENT PUBLIC INTEREST RE-
SEARCH GROUP (OSPIRG)
P. O. Box 1364
Portland, Oregon 97207
(503) 754-2101

MINNESOTA PUBLIC INTEREST RESEARCH
GROUP (MPIRG)
2118 University Ave., S. E.
Minneapolis, Minnesota 55414
(612) 376-7554

PUBLIC INTEREST RESEARCH GROUP
P. O. Box 28018
Central Station
Washington, DC. 20005
Attention: Donald Ross
(202) 833-9700